Reaction

Anger Management for Parents,
Using Positive Parenting Techniques

E. Avital

REACTION

Anger Management for Parents, Using Positive Parenting Techniques

First Edition

Copyright © 2022 E. Avital

Formatted by Saqib Arshad

Printed in the United States of America

TABLE OF CONTENTS

INTRODUCTION

If you are patient in one moment of anger, you will escape a hundred days of sorrow.

- CHINESE PROVERB

As humans, we are a constant flurry of emotions. We can navigate feelings of joy, anger, frustration, and hope in a single day. We consistently react to our environment. Everything that happens around us has a significant effect on how we feel and how we cope with those feelings.

There are also times when things get out of hand. There are situations where we let our emotions get the better of us. I'm sure you've been there before. I have been there many times myself. However, the issue is not feeling the way we do. The problem is allowing our feelings to dictate our reactions. Unfortunately, losing control for a moment can lead to negative consequences.

I'm here to tell you that it's all right to feel like you do. It's perfectly fine to go through a rollercoaster of emotions. I'm also here to tell you that, as parents, we shouldn't be afraid of our feelings. However, the challenge is harnessing our emotions to avoid a hundred days of sorrow.

I have worn many hats in my life.

I have been a student.

I have been a teacher.

I have been a counselor.

Most importantly, I am a mother.

I have learned so much about what makes us tick in each situation. I have also learned what ticks us off.

You see, being a parent is not easy. No one ever said it would be. There are many situations where our children trigger our emotions. We often worry about harming our children if we lose control, and rightfully so. However, we tend to suppress our feelings if we don't know what to do about them. We bottle them up or try to run away from them.

Let me tell you that is not a good solution.

In life, we must learn to cope with our emotions. We owe it to our kids to find the best way to handle our feelings, especially when children push the wrong buttons.

We've all been there before.

A tough day. Bills to pay. The harsh realities of adulthood. Then, we come home to a wonderful family. Except there are times when they aren't so wonderful.

Suddenly, everything comes crashing down like a ton of bricks.

Introduction

I know what that's like. But I also know what it's like to find the right path toward coping with everything life throws at us. For me, it was embracing mindfulness.

When I discovered mindfulness, I found a path toward managing my emotions. I opened a new world of possibilities. I was no longer a prisoner to the world around me. Sure, there isn't much I can do about the things around me, but I can certainly manage how I feel about them.

As I embraced mindfulness, I used it to help my teaching role. I was much more adept at handling my feelings in the classroom. I could better process my emotions, mainly when my little angels flew off the handle.

My experience has allowed me to help others find a balance in their lives. I have spoken to many parents about my experience and techniques. Many have also found a way to manage their feelings. Together, we have uncovered effective ways to cope with the stress that comes with everyday life.

Now, I am here to share my experience with you, too.

I am not writing this book because I want to preach how wonderful being mindful can be. Of course, being mindful is great. There are many great books out there on the subject. But I would like to focus on what it's like to use mindfulness in parenting.

I'm sure you know there's no manual on parenting. Otherwise, it would be the world's number one bestseller (after the bible, maybe). The truth is that we all learn to be parents as we go along. That is why we owe it to ourselves to share our experiences. We need to share our lessons on what works and what doesn't. Most importantly, we can reflect on how we can better handle our feelings daily.

Throughout this book, we will focus on how to manage our anger and frustration. We will begin by discussing anger, especially concerning our relationships with our children. We will focus on what triggers it and how we can recognize its onset. Then, we will focus on children's developmental stages. As a mother, I am keenly focused on learning about them as much as possible. I have shared my learning with parents, colleagues, and others. And now, I want to share my perspective with you here.

I want to stress that the core of my discussion with you focuses on positive parenting methods. These methods aim to eliminate many of the stressors that come with being a parent and can help you cope with anger. With time, you'll be able to avoid it altogether.

Now, please keep in mind that this isn't about suppressing anger. It's about nipping it in the bud before it becomes an issue!

We will also discuss everything you need to know about events that trigger anger. We will discuss what they are and how you can recognize them. In doing so, you will learn to understand better how these triggers unleash episodes of anger. As we dig deep into our psyche, we will uncover practical tools you can use to cope with anger, remove yourself from the situation, and regain focus. We'll discuss techniques such as mindfulness, relaxation, and breathing to help you get back on track.

Moreover, we will focus on how you can reconnect with your children, especially after a fight. I know this can be an excruciating point for all of us. So, I would like to share my experience with you on this crucial point.

We will also focus on what children need as they progress through their developmental phases. As we drill down on each stage, we'll discuss how we can improve our communication by enhancing our understanding of what makes our kids tick. This understanding leads to a responsive approach. As a result, we'll be moving away from a traditional reactive one. Ultimately, become more attuned with your positive emotions (happiness, calmness, love) instead of letting the negative get a grip on you.

There is one crucial topic I can't wait to discuss with you: self-care. We will focus on how self-care is essential to your efforts as an effective parent. After all, how can you pour from an empty cup? We need to keep it full, so you can shower your kids with all the love they need.

In the last section of this book, we will focus on how to connect with your child at a deeper level. We will discuss how you can take your relationship to a new level through meaningful communication. As your communication builds, you will find that your bond will also strengthen. Improving communication and strengthening bonds will lead you toward a calm, happy home.

I hope you are as excited as I am!

I know there is a lot to cover. So, I don't want to waste any time. We have a fantastic journey ahead of us.

Let's get on with it, then.

CHAPTER 1

Getting a Grip on Anger

Anger doesn't solve anything. It builds nothing, but it can destroy everything.

- LAWRENCE DOUGLAS WILDER

Anger is a highly destructive force. It's like a hurricane that consumes everything in its path. Anger is incapable of building anything. It can destroy your life in seconds.

Do you think I am overreacting?

How many crimes have you heard of that people commit in a moment of rage?

Indeed, allowing rage to control your life can lead to tragic moments of loss and suffering. This harsh reality requires us to get a grip on anger. Even small, seemingly insignificant outbursts can add up over time. These outbursts may eventually cause you to lose control.

Once you lose control, anything can happen.

In this chapter, we're going to take a look at what anger is. We'll take a deep dive into our triggers, and most importantly, we'll talk about how we can spot anger before it controls our behaviors.

Defining Anger

The Merriam-Webster dictionary defines anger as "a strong feeling of displeasure and usually of antagonism."[i]

Wow, there's a lot to unpack there.

Firstly, anger is a "strong feeling of displeasure." Thus, we can first ascertain that anger stems from something that causes us to feel displeasure or discomfort. So, think about the last time you got angry. What feeling of displeasure caused you to get upset?

Was it a rude employee somewhere?
Was it someone cutting you off in traffic?
Was it something that happened at work?
Perhaps all of the above. But what if it's something related to your children?

We've all been there, right? An unexpected tantrum or unruly behavior. Unfortunately, a minor issue may be enough to pull the linchpin on your temper.

Generally speaking, anger stems from a situation that evokes a sensation of discomfort. Instead of being placed in a comfortable situation, rage emerges from being shoved out of our comfort zone. Berkowitz et al. (1999) highlight that anger largely depends on our emotional state. In other words, an unpleasant situation may be enough to send you over the edge if you're already feeling uncomfortable.[ii]

The second element in Merriam-Webster's definition is "antagonism." So, what exactly is antagonism? In essence, antagonism refers to "opposition." So, this term tells us that anger emerges when we face opposition. This isn't the type of opposition you face when you enter a competition. This is the type we face when we don't get our way.

Does that ring a bell?

We generally get upset when things don't go our way. We may even lose our temper when we don't get what we want or miss out on something important.

Think about it this way:

How would you feel if the promotion you wanted was given to someone else? Naturally, you would be upset. You might not lose your cool if the rise went to someone truly deserving. But what if the promotion went to someone you know didn't deserve it?

Would that flip you out?

Most people would lose their cool, for sure. After all, imagine working hard to get that promotion, and then you suddenly have the rug pulled from under you.

What about an issue at home?

Suppose your child asks for your phone. You say no. And... bam! They are on the floor, crying their lungs out.

Automatically, you're hit with opposition. The opposition emerges from your unmet expectations.

Let's face it. We deal with opposition all the time. We run into a traffic jam when we're late. We have to pay bills when we're short on cash. We get the third degree from our bosses when a gazillion things already stress us out.

Yes, that's the antagonism I'm talking about.

Back to Berkowitz et al. In a 2004 paper, Berkowitz stated that "unpleasant conditions" or "social stresses" cause feelings of anger. Moreover, the paper describes that "decidedly aversive conditions are a major spur to anger."[iii].

All right, that means anything "unpleasant" or "stressful" leads to anger.

Fair enough.

But this is what I would like you to focus on: there are a plethora of unpleasant situations we face daily. What about "social stresses?" We could make a grocery list of social stresses. The fact is that we are constantly thrust into unpleasant, uncomfortable, and painful situations. Sadly, there is very little we can do about them. We have very little control over many of the most vexing problems in life.

So, if there's very little we can do to control our environment, what can we do?

Benjamin Franklin once said, "*Anger is never without reason, but seldom with a good one.*" Old Ben was absolutely right. We always have a reason for getting angry, but we don't always have a good one. We tend to get mad over situations that don't warrant our wasted energy.

Yes, that's right. I said it. Anger is wasted energy.

Anger is unproductive.

Anger is destructive.

Do you know what the worst part is? Anger destroys you and no one else. Unless you actively hurt someone else (which we don't want you to do) or destroy an external object, anger destroys you little by little. It whittles away at your mental, emotional, and physical well-being. It eventually gnaws at your sanity until you lose grip on reality.

The biggest question we must ask ourselves is why we get angry in the first place. I mean, it's OK to get upset when things don't go our way. But it's a different thing to fly off the handle completely. Trust me, the waiter messing up your order is not the root cause of your outburst. That was merely the event that sent you over the edge. To fully understand what fuels your anger, you must look within yourself. External factors only catalyze feelings of anger.

Causes of Anger

So, the time has come to examine the causes of anger. Indeed, there are a seemingly infinite number of reasons for anger issues. The root causes of anger issues range from unresolved childhood issues to prolonged exposure to stress. Oh, and we can also throw in singular traumatic events.

Yes, there is any number of reasons that drive anger. But we must learn to differentiate annoyance from rage.

How so?

Think about this situation:

You've told your kids numerous times to pick up their toys. However, they keep leaving them lying around the floor. It's incredibly annoying to walk into your living room with toys everywhere. After all, you never know when you might step on something and hurt yourself.

One day, after telling your kids to pick up their toys for the millionth time, you walk into the living room while on the phone. You step on a toy and slip.

What would be the most appropriate reaction in that situation?

If you're having a good day, this type of incident might be nothing more than a minor nuisance.

But what if you're stressed out and in a bad mood? This incident might drive you over the edge. You could very well give in to the rage you've already built up.

I'm not saying that going bananas would be an appropriate reaction. I am saying that it would make sense for you to lose your cool in that situation, especially if you've had the worst day ever.

But here's the deal: the key is to spot the causes of an outburst. So, let's focus on two aspects.

First, I'd like you to think about the last time you got angry. It could have been today (and perhaps that's why you've decided to read this book). It could have been last week. It could have been days or weeks ago.

Next, think about what caused you to get upset. Be honest. Think about the circumstances that caused you to lose your cool. Chances are there was more than one cause.

Now, think about your reaction. Did you explode? Did you keep it together? How did you feel after the situation was over?

Lastly, reflect on how you felt afterward. Be honest with yourself. Please take the time to reflect on the situation and your reaction. If you think you could have handled things differently, I would like to encourage you to explore how you could have handled the situation better. If you feel satisfied with how you reacted, I will enable you to explore alternative ways you could have responded. Perhaps there was another way to approach the situation.

Please remember that there may be more profound, underlying causes of anger issues. These causes may have a root in physiological aspects beyond external motivators (such as an annoying co-worker). Moreover, anger issues may stem from other psychological factors. Therefore, it's crucial to dissect how these psychological issues could trigger feelings of anger or rage.

Harmon-Jones (2007) suggests that anger is an adaptive function. In that regard, anger results from our psyches attempting to adjust to other underlying situations. [iv] We're indeed talking about insidious causes that go unnoticed for years. Unfortunately, these causes only light after anger issues have become too much to handle.

So, let's begin by taking a closer look at two specific factors that can directly lead to anger issues.

Addiction

Addiction is a powerful force that drives a wide range of emotions. Addiction can trigger feelings of anxiety, aggression, and anger. Addiction and anger form a vicious cycle that can be extremely difficult to escape. Specifically, anger fuels addiction as individuals seeks solace in substance abuse such as alcohol and drugs. Moreover, people without anger issues may develop them due to substance abuse.[v] As a result, addictions serve as an escape valve that does not always provide relief.

Mental health issues

Mental health issues can become a severe catalyst for anger management concerns. Conditions such as anxiety, depression, or obsessive-compulsive disorder (OCD) can trigger outbursts. A 2011 study showed a correlation between anger and OCD. But here's the real kicker: anger issues escalated in test subjects with some type of history, such as substance abuse, mental health concerns, or emotional trauma.[vi]

Other conditions that may trigger anger issues include attention deficit hyperactivity disorder (ADHD), oppositional defiant disorder (ODD), bipolar disorder, and intermittent explosive disorder (IED). IED is an important yet relatively unknown cause of anger problems. IED is characterized by actions such as temper tantrums, constant arguing, fighting, physical violence, or breaking objects..[vii]

Researchers believed that IED was a rare occurrence. With modern testing protocols, psychologists have identified IEDs much more effectively. Additionally, studies suggest that IED correlates with poor impulse control..[viii]

Dealing with mental health issues is a serious business. Anyone struggling with these conditions needs to assess their options. Often, treatment such as counseling or therapy significantly alleviates anger issues. There is no shame in asking for help. Getting help is the first step toward finding harmony in life.

Please note that addictions and mental health issues tend to be quite extreme. After all, not everyone deals with these issues. Nevertheless, they are worth considering. But it's also worth considering common causes. These causes may go unnoticed. So, we must set our sights on them.

Social stressors

Social stressors are a common cause of anger issues in all of us. I mean, think about all of the social issues swirling around us daily. I know we could spend the entire day listing everything that affects us. Everything from traffic to the economy can cause significant amounts of stress. While these stressors may not constitute the root cause of anger issues, they can certainly contribute to fostering feelings of discomfort and unpleasantness.

Trauma

We cannot ignore the role that trauma plays in our lives. For instance, post-traumatic stress disorder (PTSD) can become a significant factor in driving anger issues. People dealing with PTSD are prone to "anger attacks" as they attempt to cope with their experiences.[ix] Please remember that anger is a response that our minds use to adjust to our environment and circumstances. It, therefore, makes sense to assume that the psyche uses anger as a regulatory mechanism. The same goes for grief. One of the essential stages of grief, mainly when dealing with a significant loss, is anger.[x] Anger becomes a way for the mind to process a loss. Eventually, anger subsides in most individuals. For some people, anger never truly goes away due to unresolved issues. Grief may become an intensifier of anger when it compounds with other traumas.

As you can see, there are various causes driving anger. While some are more serious than others, we should not disregard any of them. When left unattended, even the most miniature sources of irritation can become powerful forces.

Understanding what sets off the fuse that explodes the anger bomb is crucial. So, we must drill down into what triggers our outbursts. As Buddha once said, "Holding on to anger is like drinking poison and expecting the other person to die." Indeed, anger is a poison circulating in our veins. The problem is often spotting it once it's too late.

When we learn to spot anger before it's too late, we allow ourselves the chance to avoid huge mistakes. Ambrose Bierce once remarked, "Speak when you are angry, and you will make the best speech you will ever regret."

How many times have we said things we regret just because we were angry at the time?

Plenty of us has lost jobs, clients, relationships, and even our dignity by lashing out of anger. Spotting the triggers that cause outbursts gives us a fighting chance against rage. Let's examine these triggers in closer detail.

Defining Triggers

Triggers are things, events, or people that cause an abrupt change in mood. Emotional, psychological, or mental health triggers cause an impression on the psyche that elicits a specific reaction.[xi] In this case, we're looking at the triggers that unleash outbursts of anger or rage.

Triggers are everywhere. They can be widespread occurrences, such as car horns. Triggers can also be specific conditions, such as words or phrases. These so-called "trigger words" can unleash an individual's fury. For example, victims of bullying often experience anger attacks when they hear the words bullies use to taunt them.

Simply put, emotional triggers attack our impulse control abilities. Triggers are effective based on how well we can control our impulses.

Consider this situation:

You are stressed out following a terrible day at work. You leave the office late and run into rush hour traffic. As traffic grinds to a halt, everyone blares their car horns out of frustration. In this context, your impulse control is much weaker, given the overall context of your day.

In contrast, your impulse control may become much stronger when you're in a good mood. For instance, suppose you've had a wonderful day. Everything has gone your way. When you leave the office, you run into some traffic. As everyone else begins to pound their horns, you turn up the volume on your favorite song.

Do you see the difference in both scenarios?

Ultimately, psychological triggers challenge or antagonize our impulse control. People with very little tolerance tend to show inadequate impulse control.[xii] These are the folks that snap at the slightest provocation. The challenge we face is comprehending how emotional triggers challenge our impulse control. Once we figure out how our impulse control reacts to these triggers, we can better equip ourselves to handle stressors in our environment. Ultimately, we can improve our control over most of our reactions.

Types of Emotional Triggers

Various types of occurrences can trigger a negative emotional response:

Rejection

Rejection can come in many forms. It refers to someone's refusal to engage with us. A classic example is social rejection, such as children refusing to play with each other. Prolonged exposure to rejection can lead to pent-up emotions leading to anxiety, depression, and anger attacks..[xiii]

Betrayal

Betrayal can cause significant trauma in a person's life. The perceived notion of being fooled, deceived, or double-crossed can lead to intense feelings of resentment. At first, these feelings may not necessarily subside. However, these feelings can easily fester to a point where they become an underlying source of anger.

Challenge

The opposition of any kind can trigger anger attacks or temper tantrums. Challenges don't necessarily mean having someone physically threaten you. In fact, "no" is the most common trigger word. For instance, customer service agents are trained to avoid using the word "no" when speaking to customers. For some folks, the mere utterance of "no" represents such a considerable challenge that they instantly lose their cool.

Helplessness

For some people, helplessness causes them to lash out. When people feel there is nothing they can do about a situation, anger becomes a coping mechanism. Think about feeling helpless in the workplace. For example, people with horrible bosses become bitter and angry, especially when they can't leave their job because they need it. In such situations, anger becomes an escape valve for these feelings of pain, anxiety, and resentment.[xiv]

Neglect

We often associate neglect with abandonment. For instance, children who suffer neglect from their parents (physical or emotional) tend to grow up with feelings of resentment and bitterness. These feelings morph into anger, physical violence, or anger attacks. In the worst cases, people in these circumstances turn to substance abuse as a coping mechanism. When people find themselves in toxic relationships, anger almost always becomes the go-to escape valve. Consequently, future instances of rejection or disapproval may unleash feelings of rage.[xv]

As we get more familiar with emotional triggers, we can summarize them with one word: experience. Often, we carry around feelings associated with past events. Many of these feelings don't necessarily surface. They lay beneath the surface like most of an iceberg's mass. We see the noticeable emotional reactions, but we don't comprehend what drives these situations. Even when we strive to keep an open mind, doing so can be pretty challenging.

In her book Parent-Infant Psychodynamics, Joan Raphael-Leff puts the power of the past into perspective with this thought: "We all approach new situations with old trepidations, and, clearly, the more traumatic the previous situation, the greater the anxiety about current ones."[xvi]. Indeed, the past can have a powerful effect on our psyche. This effect is potent when we've been through a traumatic experience. Please bear in mind that "traumatic" doesn't necessarily mean abuse. It could practically be anything.

Consider this situation:

I met someone who'd been in a car accident as a child. This traumatic experience caused her to get extremely anxious while driving. Every time she got behind the wheel, her anxiety spiked. This effect reduced her tolerance significantly. As a result, she struggled to keep her cool when her kids acted up in the car.

As you can see, a seemingly unrelated issue can profoundly affect you years later. So, I would invite you to consider your past. Ask yourself if there is anything that might affect how you view your present situation based on past experiences. Perhaps something is bubbling beneath the surface. You only need to put your finger on it to see it.

Social Triggers

Social triggers are everywhere. We've mentioned situations such as traffic, rude people, and or even social injustice. However, spotting how social stimuli affect you generally boils down to your overall disposition.

How so?

Social triggers can significantly affect you depending on your overall mood. So, should we avoid unpleasant situations as much as possible?

On the whole, yes. However, that isn't always possible. Therefore, the challenge is to manage social triggers around us so they don't control our lives. Maxime Legacé, the founder of WisdomQuotes, offers this insight, *"The smarter you get, the more you realize anger is not worth it."* This statement holds when it comes to social triggers. After all, there is very little we can do to control the environment. So, there is no sense in getting upset about it. We can't afford to waste our precious energy on things we cannot change or control.

So, I would like to challenge you here. I would like you to think about how social situations affect your outlook on yourself. If you find yourself raging about the weather, traffic, your boss, and so on, think about how these situations genuinely affect you. Chances are they have little influence over your life. Please take the time to let go of these situations. Stop letting them get to you. Instead, focus on what truly matters. You'll find that the wiser you get, the more you realize that so many things are not worth it. Anger is one of them.

How Triggers Affect Us

Thus far, we've outlined several triggers. These triggers float around us constantly. They come and go as circumstances change. So, the question is, why don't all stimuli affect us the same way?

Let's think about it for a minute.

If all triggers affected us similarly, we'd be a raging mess. We'd be seething all the time, ready to destroy everything around us.

The truth is that triggers are unique to all of us. Some triggers hit us harder than others. Some triggers may seem impossible to stop, no matter how hard we try. The worst part is that we have no control over some of these triggers.

An excellent 1997 study. [xvii] shed light on some fascinating findings. A total 0f 747 American and Russian participants self-reported anger episodes. Here's what the researchers found were the most common circumstances:

- Most incidents of anger happen at home.
- These episodes generally occur in the afternoon or evening.
- Outbursts take place on all days of the week.
- Incidents result from unexpected actions from a loved or liked person.

Yikes!

There's a lot to go over here.

First, the researchers found that most anger incidents occurred at home. Does that sound familiar? Now, you might be thinking about why we would be more prone to anger at home than in the workplace.

You see, the situation is not that we are more prone to anger at home than at the office. If anything, the workplace is the ideal location for lighting the fuse. The difference is that we are more prone to *releasing* anger at home than in the workplace.

How so?

Think about it for a second. What would happen if you went ballistic in your workplace? You might get the boot if you lose your cool, especially in front of your boss. So, we don't have much choice. We either keep it together or risk getting canned.

In contrast, we have a lot more freedom at home. We don't necessarily face direct consequences such as getting fired. Nevertheless, we do have harsh effects. The only difference is that these consequences take time to manifest themselves. But when they do, they can be disastrous.

Also, the 1997 study mentions that episodes occurred in the afternoon or evening. When you think about it, it makes perfect sense. I mean, why would you snap early in the morning? Generally speaking, we feel much better after a night's sleep. There is, of course, the possibility that you've had a rough night. In the evening, though, we've been through an entire day's worth of antagonism. So, it makes sense to have a short fuse, especially when we get home from work.

Do you see a pattern emerging here?

The study also mentions that participants reported incidents throughout the week. This reporting includes the weekend. So, you think you're far more chill on the weekend than during the week? It might indeed be true. But that doesn't mean you're entirely stress-free on the weekends. There is still any number of potential triggers out there that could cause you to lose your cool. Think about having a bad experience at the mall or getting bad news. These events could quickly happen on the weekend, ruining your good mood.

Lastly, the study indicates that participants reported these incidents involving a loved or liked person. In other words, we're talking about friends and family.

See, here's the thing: people you don't care about are far less likely to antagonize you than those you love and care about.

Let's process that for a second.

A stranger cutting you off on the highway does not have the same effect as having a loved one disappoint you somehow. I mean, you will most likely never see this driver again in your life. However, you must deal with your loved one's actions and attitudes whether you want to or not.

Please remember that we hold our friends and family to a higher standard. We see them in a completely different light. After all, it's hard for a stranger to disappoint us. We don't know who they are, so they can't fail our expectations.

In contrast, our loved ones mean everything to us. Our loved ones open the door for rejection, betrayal, disappointment, antagonism, helplessness, or neglect. It's also worth mentioning that our loved ones may commit these actions unwittingly.

Yes, that's right.

Our loved ones disappoint us, not because they mean to. They disappoint us because we believe they haven't met our expectations.

Do you see where I'm going with this?

Suppose your kids bring home their report cards. Even though they passed all their classes, they didn't get the grades you hoped for.

That's pretty disappointing, right?

I suppose it would be if your kids coasted through the entire term without putting much effort into their classwork. But what if they tried their best and still didn't get the grades you wanted them to?

Would that be a disappointment?

I can tell you that I celebrate my students' efforts regardless of the outcome. I want them to try their very best. If they don't achieve a particular grade or mark, that's fine! They'll do it next time.

Final Thoughts

By now, I hope to have established one crucial element: anger is based on your perception of events. Of course, there are things we must certainly be upset about, such as social injustice. However, we must step back and truly analyze why we get upset. Chances are that e things you most often get angry about are based on your perception of the situation around you. So, the time has come for you to challenge your perception of the things that trigger your anger.

I'm here to remind you that you're not alone on this journey. Like you, I've been through this situation, as well as many other parents. Don't forget you're not the only one. We all go through it at one point or another. Therefore, we must take the time to figure out the best way to get a grip on our emotions, what triggers them, and how we can better manage our feelings.

In the following chapters, we'll dive deeply into how triggers affect your overall reaction to the circumstances around you. Specifically, we'll discuss individual triggers and how they permeate your responses to your children's behavior. So, please don't touch that dial because we have lots more coming your way!

---

[i] Merriam-Webster (2022). Definition of Anger. Available at: https://www.merriam-webster.com/dictionary/anger

[ii] Berkowitz, L. (1999). Anger.

[iii] Berkowitz, L., & Harmon-Jones, E. (2004). Toward an understanding of the determinants of anger. *Emotion, 4*(2), 107.

[iv] Harmon-Jones, E. A., & Harmon-Jones, C. (2007). Anger: Causes and components.

[v] Baharvand, P., & Malekshahi, F. (2019). Relationship between anger and drug addiction potential as factors affecting the health of medical students. *Journal of Education and Health Promotion, 8.*

[vi] Painuly, N. P., Grover, S., Mattoo, S. K., & Gupta, N. (2011). Anger attacks in obsessive compulsive disorder. *Industrial psychiatry journal, 20*(2), 115–119. https://doi.org/10.4103/0972-6748.102501

[vii] Coccaro, E. F. (2012). Intermittent explosive disorder as a disorder of impulsive aggression for DSM-5. *American Journal of Psychiatry, 169*(6), 577-588.

[viii] *Ibid.*

[ix] Novaco, R. W. (2010). Anger and psychopathology. In *International handbook of anger* (pp. 465-497). Springer, New York, NY.

[x] Kübler-Ross, E., & Kessler, D. (2009). The five stages of grief. In *Library of Congress Catalogin in Publication Data (Ed.), On grief and grieving* (pp. 7-30).

[xi] Kashdan, T. B., Goodman, F. R., Mallard, T. T., & DeWall, C. N. (2016). What triggers anger in everyday life? Links to the intensity, control, and regulation of these emotions, and personality traits. *Journal of Personality, 84*(6), 737-749.

[xii] Lochman, J. E., Barry, T., Powell, N., & Young, L. (2010). Anger and aggression. In *Practitioner's guide to empirically based measures of social skills* (pp. 155-166). Springer, New York, NY.

[xiii] Novaco, *Ibid.*

[xiv] *Ibid.*

[xv] *Ibid.*

[xvi] Raphael-Leff, J. (2005). Parent–infant psychodynamics: Wild things, mirrors and ghosts. *Infant Observation, 8*(3), 291-292.

[xvii] Kassinove, H., Sukhodolsky, D. G., Tsytsarev, S. V., & Solovyova, S. (1997). Self-reported anger episodes in Russia and America. *Journal of Social Behavior and Personality, 12*(2), 301-324.

CHAPTER 2
Watching Children Flourish

Children do not move, think or speak in a straight line, and neither does imagination or creativity. But sadly, our standardized pathways of education do.

- VINCE GOWMON

Children are magical beings. They emerge from a tiny collection of cells in a marvelous creation. We don't always realize our privilege to witness one of life's authentic miracles.

On the surface, it isn't always easy to see how children grow and develop. Under the hood, there are thousands of processes firing on all cylinders. These processes allow kids to build the skills they need to live meaningful lives.

If you thought that children grew in linear, predictable patterns, you might be surprised to find they don't. Children never grow in a straight line. There are plenty of twists and turns along the way. Nevertheless, broad indicators help us determine the overarching developmental stages of a child's development.

That's what we're here to discuss.

This chapter will discuss how children's developmental paths are similar yet different. We will discuss children's main developmental stages while also focusing on the uniqueness of every child.

Before we continue, there is one thing I'd like you to keep in mind. Each child is a beautiful collection of skills and talents. They have unlimited potential, the potential to become virtually anything they wish to be. So, it is up to us to help them tap into that potential to flourish into the wonderful being they are meant to be.

A clear understanding of our children's development lets us fully grasp their behaviors and reactions. It allows us to see that our children act the way they do to communicate their needs according to their developmental stage. Knowing our children's developmental stages is like having a roadmap to our kids' psyches. This knowledge will put much of your frustration and anger at ease. By the end of this chapter, I am sure you'll see how many of your children's most challenging moments are part and parcel of their development.

Are you ready?

Let's dive right in.

Defining Developmental Stages

When discussing a child's developmental stages, it is virtually impossible to pinpoint precise moments when they transition from one phase to the next. The truth is that children move from one stage to another at different times. More often than not, each child has their own rhythm. So, we cannot expect every child to transition simultaneously.

When defining developmental stages, we must think of the big picture. These broad brushstrokes paint the main outline of a child's growth. In this regard, all children are essentially the same. The details of every child's personality are what make them truly unique.

Please bear in mind that several factors impact a child's development. These factors pertain to family and social life, their community, and the education they receive. While we cannot generalize, we can assume that some situations affect children more than others.

Consider this situation:

Children growing up in a nurturing home environment generally develop more self-confidence than those who grow up in an abusive one. This example highlights the importance of a child's surroundings in their overall development.

Renowned Swiss psychologist Jean Piaget first posited the existence of stages in a child's development. He believed that children transitioned in four broad stages to adulthood. Piaget's contributions paved the way for modern psychologists to enhance their knowledge and understanding of children's development.

It's worth highlighting that Piaget focused mainly on children's cognitive development. In other words, he focused primarily on mental and emotional development. Piaget did not focus his research on physical development. However, he did point out that physical development was crucial to ensure proper cognitive growth. [xviii]

Piaget first divided childhood development into four broad stages:

1. Sensorimotor: birth to two years.
2. Preoperational: two to seven years.
3. Concrete operational: seven to eleven years.
4. Formal operational: twelve years and over.

Each stage marks both physical and cognitive milestones. Consequently, a child cannot fully develop in each phase without both physical and mental growth occurring in sync. So, let's take a look at each stage in more detail.

Sensorimotor stage

This stage is your child's first approach to the world. Here, you have a baby just beginning to sink its teeth into the world (even if they don't have any yet). During the sensorimotor stage, children begin to discover the world around them. As a result, their senses play a crucial role in their cognitive development. Without their senses, children would be unable to engage with the world around them.

Think about this situation:

Children at this stage touch everything around them. They grab everything they see. They smell, hear, and taste everything. This stage is where children use their mouths to explore the world. Since eyesight takes some time to develop fully, children rely on all of their senses to ease their way into the world. Indeed, this stage is a truly magical one. Children uncover the amazing world around them.

Here are the main highlights of this phase:

- Children discover movement and sensations.
- Children develop essential functions such as grasping, looking, hearing and sucking.
- Children learn about the existence of objects around them.
- Children realize they are separate entities from the world around them, especially their mothers.
- Children realize the effects of their actions and the actions around them.

In short, this is the stage where everything is brand-new to a child. Therefore, it is important to surround them with as much meaningful stimulation as possible.

Preoperational stage

The preoperational stage is an exciting time because children begin to develop most of their fundamental skills. Significant milestones include walking and language. During this stage, children start to become more independent.

Here are the main highlights you can expect in this stage:

- Children begin recognizing and using symbols to represent thoughts, feelings, and objects. For instance, children associate sounds with specific items, such as barking with a dog.

- Children may display egocentric behavior. At this point, children may show selfish behavior. They may also express high levels of aggression.
- Children mainly think concretely. As a result, abstract thought, such as expressing emotions, is still tricky.

Children generally start school at this stage. So, many skills they have already developed enable them to thrive at school. However, children that do not adequately develop their skills may experience considerable difficulties in their early days at school.

Concrete operational stage

By now, children still think in very concrete terms. Nevertheless, the emergence of logic and reasoning enables children to grasp abstract concepts such as emotions. As a result, children tend to become less selfish and aggressive since they can process their feelings. Kids' linguistic and mathematical skills also make significant strides.

Here are the significant milestones to consider:

- Children show improved logic and reasoning skills.
- Children recognize shapes and dimensions around them. For example, they recognize tall, short, wide, and narrow characteristics.
- Children's thought patterns become much more organized.
- Children begin to use logic and reasoning to derive generalizations. Here, children can follow simple rules

about order and behavior (getting in line, waiting for their turn, and sharing).

As such, kids develop their understanding of feelings and begin empathizing with others. Also, children comprehend the consequences of their actions. As a result, they begin to avoid aggressive and selfish behavior in favor of sharing and socializing.

Formal Operational Stage

At this point, children have mastered the basics of maneuvering the world around them. Children have learned the most important rules regarding the world around them. They are primarily independent and require less supervision for routine tasks such as going to the bathroom, eating, getting dressed, and showering. Children also have a relatively firm grasp of their emotions. Their reasoning skills allow them to see beyond the concrete world around them.

Here are the significant milestones of this stage:

- Children develop abstract thought in hypothetical situations enabling them to improve their problem-solving skills.
- Children begin grasping abstract thoughts about moral, ethical, social, and even political issues.
- Children use deductive reasoning to go beyond generalizations and explore more specific information and data.

As children enter adolescence, their physical development may outpace their emotional and cognitive growth. Therefore, parents need to give kids the reassurance they need to navigate some of the most confusing times in their lives.

As you can see, Piaget was indeed on to something. His work paved the way for our modern understanding of children's development. However, it's easy to see that his work was largely incomplete. The idea of development essentially ending at 12 seems shortsighted. We now know that children's development continues well into the teenage years. As a result, modern psychologists have taken Piaget's groundbreaking work and retooled it to fit our current understanding of child growth and development.

The Stages of Development

When we think of development, we think of progress. As such, we can conceptualize growth as the sequence in which a child progressively becomes independent to the point where they no longer depend on their parents.[xix]

There is a lot to unpack here.

First, the thought of development revolves around the concept of "independence." As a result, children's development mainly rests in their ability to become less reliant on their parents. For some children, it takes longer than others. Some never become truly independent and rely on their parents well into adulthood. These folks are financially dependent on their parents into their forties because they can't hold down a job or run their lives.

I'm sure you've seen these situations before.

Now, this thought is not meant to be an indictment. While these cases are not as common, it's intended to show how development should foster independence so that children transition into adults. Please remember that the main objective of children's growth is to figure out how to deal with the world around them. In other words, they must acquire the tools they need to navigate the situations facing them in real life.

Consider this:

Children negotiate all the time. For instance, when children play, they must negotiate several issues, such as what games to play, taking turns, and the game's rules. Children must, therefore, develop effective negotiating skills. Otherwise, children may have difficulty engaging with other kids leading to isolation and other possible emotional consequences..[xx]

When considering your child's development, it is crucial to focus on what they will need to succeed in the world. We often think of a standard set of tools, such as learning to read and write. Nevertheless, there are specific tools that children must learn at certain points in their development. They can more easily transition from one stage to the next when they do.

Think about it this way: when a child masters the skills in one stage, they will have a much easier time with the next. This process has a snowball effect. Consequently, your child compounds the skills from one step into the next, showing a cumulative impact on their overall development.

Transitioning from Stage to Stage

Earlier, we focused on Piaget's stages of development. While helpful, we also concluded that these stages don't fully cover a child's entire story. The great news is that modern psychology has given us a much deeper understanding of a child's development stages.

Modern scholars typically divide children's development stages into five major groups. Please note that these groups do not differ from Piaget's work. If anything, these stages provide more depth to Piaget's original contributions. So, according to modern scholars, let's take a detailed look at the five stages of child development.

1. Newborn

The newborn stage is a wonderfully exciting time for children and parents. At this stage, children discover the world around them. Parents also find the amazing being their child is quickly becoming. Newborns respond to the external stimuli surrounding them for the first month. They react to sound, light, and touch. It is vital to use contact to communicate with children at this point. Since children cannot communicate through language yet, it's essential to use other types of communication, like touching, caressing, snuggling, and kissing, to show their affection..[xxi]

Children's senses quickly develop during this stage. For the first six months, their eyesight and smell begin to improve. Also, motor skills start to manifest as babies discover movement in their limbs, neck, and hands. Parents may also recognize developmental disabilities in this early stage. As such, keeping a close eye on limited physical movement or lack thereof is essential.[xxii]

Emotionally, children cry and smile. Generally, crying is the main form of communication used to indicate unpleasantness. Children also cry to tell if they want or need something. Moreover, children smile and laugh to show that something pleases them. For example, babies smile when they recognize parents, siblings, grandparents, or an object they like.[xxiii]

The newborn stage lasts for about the first three months. The first stage is a fantastic time. But it is also a critical one. Parents should strive to stimulate their children with sound, image, and touch. Doing so helps children develop their cognitive and physical capabilities leading them into infancy.

Let me share these great tips I've learned throughout my experience as a parent.

Firstly, newborns need to identify the people around them. It is, therefore, critical for parents to talk to their newborns. Babies can recognize their mothers' voices quite easily. After all, they heard their mothers speak for nine months. Fathers must also take the time to talk to their newborns. In particular, phrases like "I'm your mommy" or "I'm your daddy" go a long way toward helping newborns identify their surroundings. Showing babies objects and calling them by their names allows babies to adjust to their environment.

At this point, I encourage you to read stories to your child. Don't hesitate to show them storybook pictures as you read to them. Your baby may not be fully aware of the story's content.

Nevertheless, hearing language consistently helps turbocharge your baby's linguistic skills.

2. Infancy

Things get interesting during infancy. Infancy typically ranges from three months to a year. During this stage, babies transition from total dependency on their caregiver to becoming a bit more self-sufficient.

During infancy, babies begin to figure out movement. They can voluntarily control their arms and legs. Head and neck movement also becomes much more prominent. By six months, most children can sit independently and may even show signs of crawling.[xxiv]

Security is a key element during infancy. In addition to keeping your child safe (i.e., removing sharp objects from a child's grasp), children need freedom as they begin to move. They need their caregiver close by but not interrupting. It allows children to move freely while knowing they have someone to protect them at all times. This approach is a very effective way to develop a child's autonomy.

Infancy is also a wild time because babies love to grab everything they see. Kids this age are ready to scoop up anything that tickles their fancy. So, don't be surprised if your child suddenly snatches your glasses off your face!

Signs of developmental issues may include limited mobility or slow responsiveness. Nevertheless, children grow at different rates. So, it's always good to keep a close watch on how the child progresses throughout this stage.

3. Toddler

The toddler stage typically ranges from one to three years. Here is where things get fun! Most children begin walking at this stage. Most kids start to crawl before their first birthday. However, don't be surprised if your child stands up and starts zipping around the house before they're one.

As children develop their gross motor skills (walking, running, jumping, crawling), their cognitive skills go into overdrive. Typically, children begin articulating words around nine to twelve months. Some two-year-olds can speak complete sentences such as "I want water" or "I am hungry." While linguistic development can vary significantly from child to child, most children understand basic instructions.[xxv]

As for logic and reasoning, toddlers can perform basic logical tasks such as putting a square shape into a square hole. Toddlers also identify colors and associate sounds with objects. For example, toddlers know that dogs bark or that cars go vroom.

Developmental challenges may become more apparent at this stage. Nevertheless, providing toddlers with ample stimuli can significantly enhance their growth. Doing so can greatly help them overcome any perceived lag in their progress.[xxvi]

I encourage you to play with your toddler as much as possible. Specifically, physical activity is critical to boosting your child's motor skills. Games such as kicking a ball or picking up objects significantly give children a chance to move their bodies.

As for cognitive skills, talk to your child as much as possible. Show them pictures. Point to objects. Read to them. This time is perfect for introducing music into their lives. Most importantly, affection is critical.

4. Preschool

The preschool years (three to five) highlight children's ability to use fine motor skills (using their hands and fingers). At this stage, kids begin developing their writing and gross motor skills, such as throwing objects, catching things, kicking, standing on one foot (such as skipping), playing more complex games, and learning the basics of sports. Children also manifest artistic skills such as dancing, singing, or musical instruments. It is not uncommon to see children this age tapping on things in a rhythmic pattern..[xxvii]

Preschool kids generally start school at about four or five. Early childhood education focuses on getting children to explore the skills they need to succeed at school. Cognitively, children start recognizing symbols (letters and numbers), colors, patterns, and generalizations about rules and behavior. Children think very concretely. As a result, their limited capacity for abstract thought makes it somewhat difficult for them to express their feelings and emotions..[xxviii]

Personally, I think the preschool years are a magical time for kids. Children see an entirely new world of possibilities open to them. As they become more and more confident, children discover the wonderful world around them. I know that you, like most parents, get anxious about kids hurting themselves as they run around exploring their environment. Nevertheless, I encourage you to allow your children as much freedom as you feel appropriate so they can freely uncover everything around them. Your children will undoubtedly appreciate the space while you stand in the background, ensuring they're all right.

5. School Age

The school-age phase is a tumultuous time. Kids from six to twelve undergo several changes throughout their lives. They begin school, make new friends, engage with adults outside the family (mainly teachers), and must negotiate their interactions with other kids.

Additionally, the school-age phase is relatively complex due to the cognitive workload kids experience. After all, going to school is not easy. While most schools' curricula are gradual, kids face difficulty dealing with the various concepts they need to learn. Language and math are considerable academic challenges for most kids. That's perfectly fine as long as you can see their progress. However, kids at this stage may show the first signs of possible learning disabilities. For instance, some kids may struggle to identify and discriminate sounds, letters, and symbols. While some kids progress at different paces than others, it's always a good idea to seek help when suspecting a child may have a learning challenge.[xxix]

As kids get closer to their teenage years, they generally become more confident and self-reliant. Children have typically mastered most basic tasks (going to the bathroom, showering, getting dressed, eating). Some kids may become entirely independent. Nevertheless, it is not uncommon for kids to require their parents' support, particularly when feeling insecure about their environment. Emotional support, therefore, becomes a significant element in ensuring that children continue to develop adequately.

I encourage you to foster communication as much as possible during this stage. Being as open and available for your kids will go a long way toward helping your bridge any differences you may face. Specifically, I would urge you to approach problem-solving with honest dialog. Dedicating time to discuss problems, especially after an argument, is a great way to avoid lingering issues.

Please bear in mind that ignoring issues allows them to fester. As unresolved problems grow, they may get out of control. When that occurs, solving differences may require the intervention of a third party, such as a therapist or spiritual counselor.

An old saying goes, "a stitch in time saves nine," which is apropos. It's always best to deal with issues before they surpass your grasp.

6. Adolescence

Adolescence is tricky, mainly depending on whom you ask. Teenage years come with various challenges—for instance, the physiological changes of puberty usher in a new set of issues to deal with. For example, teens generally become fully aware of their sexuality and gender at this stage. For some teens, this may awaken confusion and insecurity. Also, some teens face identity issues such as a weak sense of belonging. [xxx]

Additionally, the teenage years bring questions about the future, like what path to pursue in college or career. Teens may also encounter peer pressure. This phenomenon may cause them to experiment with forbidden substances. As a result, unwanted consequences may emerge during this stage.

I know this stage can make anyone's blood pressure go through the roof. But please remember that maintaining open communication with your children is always the best policy. Above all, keeping an open mind and heart is critical during this stage. Being compassionate and empathetic will help you understand your child's transition from childhood to adolescence. By the end of this phase, you'll have a confident young man or lady ready to face the complexities of adulthood.

The CDC Development Milestones

The Centers for Disease Control and Prevention (CDC) have produced a handy guide called Development Milestones. These milestones help parents reference expected behaviors and actions at various stages of a child's development. While these milestones are by no means set in stone, they will serve as a roadmap on your parenting journey.

You can find the detailed guide here: https://www.cdc.gov/ncbddd/actearly/milestones/index.html.

Now, let's take a look at what you can expect at various stages in your child's development:

- **two months**. Most children show emotions by smiling. They calm down when picked up and comforted. They make various sounds in addition to crying. Their cognitive growth allows them to follow you with their eyes and react to sounds. Babies' attention span is still quite limited.

- **four months**. Babies begin uttering sounds such as "ooo" or "ahhh." They smile to get your attention. Babies move in reaction to your movements. Babies show specific responses, such as opening their mouths when hungry. Physically, children begin moving their arms voluntarily and can hold steady without much support.

- **six months**. Babies begin to laugh. They can recognize familiar faces. Children utter sounds in reaction to your sounds. Babies at this age start exploring the world with their mouths. They may also close their mouths when they are no longer hungry.

- **nine months**. Babies begin to show facial expressions to show emotions. They may become clingy or shy around strangers. Babies start to recognize their names. They begin to babble to communicate. Children at this stage often search for toys and familiar objects.

- **One year**. Children begin playing simple games. They utter their first words. They also understand basic commands such as "no." Kids at this stage can put two objects together or look for you when you hide from them. Children generally begin crawling or standing at this time.

- **Eighteen months**. Children begin to move away from you but often look back to ensure you are still there.

They can carry out basic actions such as putting their hands out to wash them. Children show curiosity for pictures in books or objects around them. They can follow basic instructions such as "sit." At this stage, children begin attempting basic actions such as drinking from a cup or scribbling with a crayon.

- **Two years**. Children recognize others' emotions, such as happiness or upset. Children can point to things they need or want. They utter basic sentences like "more please." Children can communicate with gestures and facial expressions. Cognitively, children can turn knobs and flip switches. They can also run and kick balls.

- **Three years**. Children generally calm down a few minutes after you leave (such as at school or daycare). They interact with other children at play or hold basic conversations, particularly with other kids. Kids respond to their names when called. Children can draw basic shapes and color large items. Physically, kids start becoming more independent during mealtime or when getting dressed.

- **Four years**. Children have an active imagination. They pretend to be something else, such as a superhero or an animal. They ask questions about what they want, like, "Can I have a cookie?" Children recognize danger, such as high jumps, sharp objects, or hot surfaces. They display their emotions by hugging someone sad. Cognitively, children begin to count numbers and produce letters. Physically, they can complete several tasks, such as eating without help or holding objects.

- **Five years.** Children are capable of negotiating interactions, such as taking turns. They can perform more complex tasks such as playing sports or dancing. Kids can also help around the house, like picking up toys or putting dirty laundry away. Physically, they become more independent with self-care tasks such as going to the bathroom or getting dressed. Cognitively, they can recognize concepts such as night and day. They can generally count from 1 to 5 or quite identify letters. However, they may not be able to read complete words.

Final Thoughts

Throughout this chapter, we have explored what you can expect from your children's development. We have outlined things you can keep in mind as your child grows. However, I would like to caution you about one thing: please avoid comparing one child to another. Every child is wonderfully unique. As a result, some develop specific skills slower or faster than others. Comparing children can build negative expectations.

How so?

Parents could say things like, "why can't you be more like your sister?" These comparisons can create negative feelings in a child's mind. I would encourage you to view your child as a unique being going through a singular journey. Consequently, the milestones outlined throughout this chapter serve as parameters of what you can expect. Nothing is set in stone.

Keeping an open mind is the best approach you can take with your amazingly unique kids.

The knowledge we've accrued in the chapter can help us truly understand our kids. I hope you can see that many of the most demanding situations you might face with your child are not your "fault." They're a regular part of your children's development. Therefore, I would encourage you to view your kids as beautiful beings transitioning through stages of their journey. Your job then becomes to recognize these stages and tailor your game plan. Knowing what to expect can significantly minimize frustration, anger, and anxiety.

It worked for me, and I am sure it will work for you!

In the next chapter, we'll be moving away from focusing solely on your child and shining the spotlight on you. So, don't go anywhere because there is still lots more to come!

[xviii] El'konin, D. B. (2017). Toward the problem of stages in the mental development of the child. In *Revival: Soviet Developmental Psychology: An Anthology (1977)* (pp. 538-563). Routledge.

[xix] Decker, C. A. (2020). *Child development: Early stages through age 12.* Goodheart-Willcox Company, Incorporated.

[xx] Berk, L. (2015). *Child development.* Pearson Higher Education AU.

[xxi] Berk, *Ibid.*

[xxii] *Ibid.*

[xxiii] *Ibid.*

[xxiv] *Ibid.*

[xxv] Carelli, M. G., & Cusinato, M. (2003). Stages of infancy. *International Encyclopedia of Marriage and Family Relationships, 1,* 253-258.

[xxvi] Carelli, *Ibid.*

[xxvii] *Ibid.*

[xxviii] *Ibid.*

[xxix] *Ibid.*

[xxx] Spano, S. (2004). Stages of adolescent development.

CHAPTER 3
Nip Anger in the Bud

When you get angry, they tell you count to five before you reply.
Why should I count to five? It's what happens before you count to
five, which makes life interesting.

- DAVID HARE

Count to five... count to ten... count to one thousand. Indeed, many things can happen before you start counting. But that's where the danger lies. You can say something you regret. You might cause irreparable damage. You may even change your and your child's lives forever.

While we may be unable to control getting angry, we can control our reactions. When we learn to control our reactions, we can avoid the most unpleasant parts that come with anger. That's why it is crucial to recognize the triggers that may cause the onset of anger.

In this chapter, we will talk about knowing when to nip anger in the bud. We will discuss parenting triggers in great detail.

How can understanding parenting triggers help us curb anger?

You see, this discussion is not about stopping anger. Often, trying to stop rage is like trying to stop a river from flowing. The point of recognizing parenting triggers is to avoid letting anger get the best of us.

Think about it this way:

If you know the river will flood, you seek higher ground. That's precisely what I aim to do here. There may not be much you can do to stop the river from flooding. But there is so much you can do to avoid the disastrous consequences.

When we learn to recognize these triggers effectively, we can take control of the situation. Specifically, we can defuse a problem before it gets out of hand. For instance, your children are fighting with each other over a toy. You've already had a tough day at the office, dealt with traffic, and got bad news. You're pretty close to the edge as it is. Your kids' fight is just enough to push you over the edge.

Is there much you can do to stop anger from building up?

Not much.

Is there anything you can do to control your reaction?

Yes! There is plenty you can do to avoid going off the rails. The secret here is to recognize anger as it reared its ugly head. From there, you could manage your reactions as best as possible.

Please remember that you are always in control. There is no need to feel helpless. You have, therefore, the power to keep your reactions in check. But first, it's crucial to understand how parenting triggers push your buttons.

What Are Parenting Triggers?

When we look at parenting triggers, it's helpful to see them within the broader context of your life. In other words, you don't get angry on your own. Something needs to happen for you to lose your temper. A 2018 paper sums up this point succinctly: "Certain stressors, deriving from parental or child situational or contextual domains influence parenting stress, which also accompanies difficulties in adjusting to the parenting role."[xxxi] There is so much to unpack in this quote.

First, the researchers mention stressors. As such, you don't get angry all by yourself. Even if you have underlying emotional issues (for instance, you're dealing with losing a loved one), you don't just snap at a moment's notice. There has to be something to set things off.

Second, these stressors boil down to a parental, child, or contextual domain. This statement means that any of these sources, or all three, may influence your reaction leading to the onset of anger. In the worst cases, you might be bombarded by all three.

Third, parenting stress involves difficulty adjusting to the parenting role. This statement does not mean you can't adjust to being a parent. It implies that shifting from one context to another can make it difficult to return to a parenting role. Don't worry. This situation happens all the time. For example, you're a busy professional at the office. When you get home, you take off your professional hat and put on your mothering hat. This sudden shift in mindset makes it challenging for us parents to adjust to a parenting role.

As you can see, we face stress from various sources throughout the day. Therefore, we must understand how these stressors affect our reactions and how we focus on the context around us. Since we've already discussed contextual influences (weather, traffic, work), we will focus solely on parent and child influences.

Spotting Our Reactions

Naomi Aldort, in her 2006 book *Raising Our Children, Raising Ourselves: Transforming parent-child relationships from reaction and struggle to freedom, power, and joy,* makes a fascinating point regarding our responses to our children's behavior. She asserts that we don't necessarily react to our children's expressions. Instead, our reactions are based on the difficulties we face in processing our own emotions.

Consider this:

When children cry, whine, or throw a tantrum, our reaction is not necessarily due to our children's behavior. Instead, our frustration may arise from our inability to comprehend why our children react the way they do.

Here's the Aha! Moment:

Children lack the emotional maturity to process their emotions constructively. As adults, on the other hand, we are capable of understanding our feelings and processing them as positively as we can.

Do you see where I am going with this?

A significant chunk of our frustration, anger and even disappointment stems from our inability to process our own emotions. Therefore, we need to get a grip on our feelings before we can truly handle our kids' expressions. This understanding requires introspection.

I'd like to try this exercise with you.

- Think about the last time you got angry with your child.
- Recall what happened and how your child reacted.
- From there, reflect on how you felt. Think about how your child's reaction made you feel. Were you angry? Sad? Upset? Disappointed?
- Now, think about why you felt that way. Be honest with yourself. Was it really about your child, or was it about yourself?
- Once you have reflected on the issue, take the time to think about how you could have handled things differently. There is a good chance you can think of several ways of handling the situation differently.
- Lastly, make yourself a promise. Commit to yourself that you will make an effort to handle things differently from now on.

This introspection exercise is something you want to take the time to master. It's the type of exercise that will always help you get a sense of how you're handling situations around you.

What Are the Most Common Parenting Triggers?

Triggers are everywhere. Nevertheless, we're specifically talking about parenting triggers. So, forget about other triggers (i.e., your boss, customers, traffic, neighbors) and focus solely on the triggers that affect you as a parent.

Here is a look at the most common ones:

- **Crying.** Crying can trigger the onset of anger, particularly if the child can't seem to calm down. Also, sudden crying, apparently for no reason, can become a serious trigger.
- **Whining.** Constant whining or complaining may also trigger negative emotions. While whining may not cause a sudden onset of negative emotions, it can cause such feelings to build up over time.
- **Tantrums.** There isn't much that needs to be said here. Tantrums can easily push anyone over the edge.
- **Disobedience.** This situation is a serious cause, especially if you've been warning your child consistently about paying attention, doing something, or stopping behaving in a certain way.
- **Misbehavior.** Do I need to elaborate here? Misbehavior is a significant trigger, especially when children act out in public.

- **Sibling fights**. Sibling fights can be really annoying. Dealing with this situation often requires a substantial amount of patience.
- **School**. If your child experiences issues at school, such as getting into fights, you may experience a very short fuse. As a result, it may be tough to keep a level head.

Also, please note that other triggers may be specific to your situation. Therefore, I would encourage you to try the exercise in the previous section. It would help if you recognized what triggers your emotions and when. As we've noted before, there may be specific times when triggers get to you more easily, like in the evenings after work.

How to Recognize Triggers

Recognizing triggers is no easy task. Sometimes, triggers are so subtle that you don't even know they are there. But believe me, triggers are there. So, it is critical for you to keep an eye out for the telltale warning signs that you've been triggered.

Here is a list of red flags I've encountered throughout my experience as a mother and educator.

1. A trigger has gotten to you when you feel you can't get a grip on your reaction or emotions.
2. A trigger has gotten to you when you feel profoundly hurt by something your child has said or done.
3. When you overreact or blow a situation out of proportion, a trigger has gotten to you.
4. When you lose your temper instantly, seemingly for no reason, a trigger has gotten to you.

5. A trigger has gotten to you when you feel like you've been through this before but somehow feel powerless to change your reactions.
6. A trigger has gotten to you when you are yelling, sweating, and popping veins from your forehead.
7. When you find you want to physically hurt your child, such as grabbing them by the arm or spanking them, a trigger has gotten to you.

In particular, the last red flag is of significant concern. If you ever feel the need to use physical force to "discipline" your child, it is a clear signal that you need to get a grip on your emotions and reactions. Violence is never the answer. As a result, whenever you feel like using physical force on your child, you must immediately walk away and cool down. It is always best to address the issue once you have calmed down.

Please remember that recognizing anger as soon as possible allows you to keep your emotions in check. Consequently, you vastly improve your chances of staying cool despite a highly irritating situation.

Beyond parenting triggers that stem from your child's behavior, some triggers emerge from our past.

How so?

In his book *Parenting from the Inside Out: How a deeper self-understanding can help you raise children who thrive*, Dan Siegel discusses how parents view their children from the perspective of how they were parented. In other words, we tend to react as our parents did. For example, folks who grew up in an abusive household may feel compelled to repeat the same patterns. These patterns are so subtle that they are almost imperceptible to the individual. They are clear as day to others but not to the individual.

Based on Dr. Siegel's premise, we must take the time to understand how our parents treated us. We must dissect how our parents got it right and how they got it wrong. From there, we can assess patterns that we need to change. Specifically, we can determine why our reactions may sometimes get out of control.

Of course, not everyone comes from a dysfunctional home. Persons from loving homes tend to repeat the same patterns with their children. People that grow up with loving and supportive parents generally use the same parenting approach with their children.

Now, if you didn't have loving and supporting parents, does that mean you're doomed to repeat the same patterns?

Of course not!

You see, we all have a choice. We can choose to continue unhealthy or even toxic patterns with our kids. Conversely, we can choose to break habits that negatively affect us growing up.

This choice is **yours**.

If you were fortunate to have loving and supportive parents, I would encourage you to go through your upbringing and analyze how your parents got it right. From there, you can transfer those positive patterns into your parenting style.

Ultimately, we have the power to change our reality right now! That change begins with a conscious choice to improve our children's lives more than ours. I know that's what you want for your kids. Otherwise, we wouldn't be having this discussion right now.

Nipping Triggers in the Bud

Now that we have taken a close look at triggers, it's crucial to discuss how to nip them in the bud. We aim to ensure they no longer take control of us. We want to ensure that we're always in the driver's seat. As such, I've put together a handy reference section that will enable you to take charge of triggers for good.

In this section, you will find helpful tips and strategies to deal with triggers once and for all. I assure you that once you're done with this section, your perspective on anger will never be the same again.

The Anger Iceberg

Anger, like an iceberg, has far more than meets the eye. The visible portion of an iceberg is only about 10% of its total mass. Similarly, anger's visible portion is a fraction of what truly lies beneath the surface. In fact, anger is the final consequence of several underlying issues.

A 2020 study looked deeply into the "anger iceberg" phenomenon from a counseling perspective. This study underscores the fact that anger is not an isolated situation. Quite the contrary, anger is the consequence of any stressors surrounding the individual. In particular, this fascinating study looked at the incidence of burnout as a factor leading to anger issues. The study's findings show that burnout is a good predictor of anger management issues. [xxxii]

You can scan the QR code to view the iceberg.

As you can see, the anger iceberg shows how anger is not a random occurrence in ordinary people. Unless someone suffers from a mental health condition, the unexpected onset of anger is rare. Therefore, we must look closely at what lies beneath the surface.

The anger iceberg holds the following feelings beneath its surface:

- Disappointment
- Stress
- Embarrassment
- Overwhelming situations
- Loneliness
- Hurt
- Jealousy
- Frustration
- Grief
- Insecurity

- Helplessness
- Shame
- Anxiety
- Fear
- Hunger
- Fatigue
- Guilt
- Threat

The anger iceberg theory doesn't mean you can experience all these feelings. The theory states that even one of these feelings may be enough to predispose you to anger. Even if you are well-adjusted, being under significant stress may be enough to turn your sunny disposition into a somber outlook.

I would encourage you to consider how many of these feelings may play a role in your life. Perhaps they affect you well beneath the surface. Maybe you haven't even paid attention to them. But they are there. These issues could lurk around, prodding at your feelings when you least expect it.

So, here is an exercise that I would like you to try. It's a simple one: journaling.

Journaling is a great exercise you can do with minimal setup. You can use a paper notebook, a computer, or your phone. The aim is to chronicle your feelings. If you have a good day, write down why it's a good day. If you have a terrible one, explore why it's been a bad day. The aim is to detect patterns in your feelings. For example, journaling every day may reveal feelings of disappointment or frustration. Perhaps everything is going well in your life, but you're tired and burned out.

On the surface, you may not be able to spot any of these feelings. But as you jot down your thoughts, you'll see patterns emerging.

That's the power of journaling. Please start today. You don't need to write pages and pages of thoughts. Beginning with a paragraph is one to get the ball rolling. From there, you can uncover profound insights into your life and feelings.

From reactions to response

Now that we've warmed up let's dig deeper into our emotions. Understanding what lies beneath anger (as explained by the anger iceberg theory) helps us get a clear sense of what might be unconsciously fueling our reactions.

The next step on our journey is to isolate the precise triggers causing our reactions. With practice, we will learn to monitor our emotions and transition from reacting to responding. While there could be any number of triggers causing us to feel rage, it doesn't do us very much if we don't pinpoint the real culprits. Here is a beautiful exercise that you can do to help you identify the insidious villain causing your negative emotions.

Once you've got the worksheet in front of you, let's go through each section to understand how it can help you.

The worksheet has three main sections. Each section builds on the previous one. So, please take the time to fill out each before moving on. Doing so will make the exercise genuinely effective.

The worksheet begins with a description of the problem. There is no specific language that you must use here. All you need is to describe the situation as accurately as you can.

For example:

> "I lose control of my temper every time my kids start fighting" can be a great way to summarize the problem. Please note that this example includes a specific trigger, such as "every time my kids start fighting." If you can't put your finger on an exact trigger, try to focus on a situation.

Here is another example:

> "I often get angry easily when I come home after work."

This statement pinpoints a time when anger issues emerge. The good thing about this example is that you can isolate a time when you feel most susceptible to rage. From there, identifying the next steps comes naturally.

The following section refers to trigger categories. Here, you can list the various types of triggers within a broad category. These categories represent situations or instances where these triggers emerge. Let's take a look at them in further detail:

- **Emotional state.** Think about situations such as fatigue, stress, burnout, or grief.

- **People.** Consider people like your boss, neighbors, and family, but don't include your children.
- **Places.** This category includes work, school, traffic, or crowded locations.
- **Things.** Consider including anything that irritates you, like your neighbor's barking dogs, the noisy street where you live, and having to commute daily.
- **Thought.** Feel free to include any thoughts or ideas that upset you. Consider your opinions about your community, the economy, or the city's political situation. Additionally, consider personal items such as negative experiences, frustrations, or disappointments.
- **Activities / situations.** Jot down any specific situation or activities that cause negative feelings, such as going to meetings, dealing with certain clients, putting up with neighbors, traffic, or running the household alone.

While you don't need to fill every category, it helps if you do. You see, individual items may not necessarily get to you. But when you add them all up, they get to you significantly. Therefore, this exercise aims to help you see the big picture of stressors in your life. By the end of this section, you will have gotten a broader perspective of how everything around you has the potential to contribute to your negative feelings.

Once you have filled out your list of triggers, it's time to focus on the most significant ones. This section aims to hone in on the frequent triggers that get to you. These triggers are the ones that pose the most significant threat overall.

There are three lines for you to describe your top three triggers in as much detail as possible. Please don't hold back. Take the time to articulate your ideas in as detail as you can. Consider this example:

> "Work is really getting to me. I am stressed out and overworked. I can't concentrate on anything. When I get home, my job follows me. My boss won't leave me alone."

Tip: Include any specific examples if you can. For instance, there is an obnoxious colleague you can't be with anymore. So, you believe your job would be much better without this person. A specific example like this can go a long way toward isolating the significant causes of your negative feelings.

In the next section, we will get proactive. Here, we will describe strategies we can use to cope with these triggers. Please note that these strategies are not necessarily solutions. They are, nonetheless, ways to help you cope with the stressor.

Let's go back to our previous example. Here is a possible way to alleviate the situation:

> "I am overworked because I have taken on responsibilities that don't fit my job description. So, I will talk to my boss to ensure I can let go of some of these responsibilities to bring my overall workload down."

As you can see, the aim is to take action. Your strategies don't have to be the solution. But they must begin addressing the issue. The idea is to do something. Anything to help you avoid or reduce your exposure to the stressor. In doing so, you can begin to deny fuel to negative emotions.

The final section deals with ways to cope with an issue where there is no way you can avoid it. For instance, what can you do with your obnoxious colleague if you have no choice but to work with them daily? If the situation is so bad that you cannot stand it anymore, you may be left with no choice but to confront the colleague. You can bring up the issue with your supervisor and force the situation. Let your supervisor and your colleague know why their behavior is unacceptable. Again, this might not be the ultimate solution. But for now, you're taking matters into your own hands.

I hope you find this worksheet as helpful as I have. I've often used it myself and tried it on my friends, family, and colleagues. Every time we do this exercise, we uncover stressors we may have overlooked. So, I would encourage you to give this worksheet a try. I am sure you'll be glad you did.

Three Quick Techniques to Help you Manage Anger

All right, so what happens when the action gets hot and heavy? What can you do to keep a level head when tempers flare?

I know staying calm when you're caught up in the heat of the moment can be challenging. So, here are three quick, simple techniques you can use to keep cool, especially when you're in the thick of things.

1. Take a timeout

There is nothing wrong with walking away when you're angry. I've done it hundreds of times. When I catch myself feeling upset, I walk away. I turn around and remove myself from the situation. Leaving a hostile situation doesn't make you a coward. If anything, it makes you strong.

Do you know how hard it is to let something go?

For example, imagine your child knocked something over and broke it. Instead of engaging in the situation right then, you can remove yourself from the case. If your child is safe, communicate to them, you need a moment for yourself and take a timeout to regroup. Once you've cleared your head, you can come back and explain to your child why their behavior was inappropriate. Your child will greatly appreciate you explaining why their actions were wrong instead of berating them.

2. Take a deep breath

Yes, we've heard this one before. But how often do we do it?

Now, here's something you might not have thought of. When we get angry, our blood pressure rises, our pulse rate spikes and the fight-or-flight response kicks in. More often than not, we stop breathing. Our breath becomes shallow. This condition means that our brains don't get enough oxygen. As a result, your cognitive ability becomes impaired at that moment.[xxxiii]

Do you see where I am going with this?

Taking a deep breath is an excellent way for you to ensure your brain gets enough oxygen. Consequently, your entire nervous system settles back down instead of overdrive. Once you've regrouped, you can address the situation as needed.

3. Take a moment to think

Anger has a way of making us act instinctively. There is no surprise there. As humans, evolution has wired us to make snap judgments. Our ancestors were faced with them all the time. They needed to make instant decisions, or else they'd become some predator's lunch.

In our modern world, we must get into the habit of thinking. We must take a moment to think about our actions, especially when we get highly emotional. I would encourage you to use your timeout to think about how you can respond to the situation. You don't need hours to ponder your next move. A couple of minutes is enough to avoid disastrous consequences. For example, if your child has spilled something, take a timeout. Then, take a deep breath. After, take a moment to think of a solution. Leaving a mess on the floor for a few minutes will not harm anyone. I promise! Perhaps cleaning up the mess together will be a learning experience for your child.

The Consequences of Our Actions

As we draw this chapter to a close, I'd like to reflect on the consequences of our actions. Indeed, we hold enormous power in relationships with our kids. We are in complete control of the relationship all the time. Our kids depend on us for practically everything, especially at a younger age. Therefore, we owe it to them to ponder the consequences our actions may have on them.

So, I'd like to leave you with one more exercise. I'd like you to use your empathy. Think about how your child feels within your relationship. Put yourself in their place.

Can you get a sense of how they feel?

Are they secure?

Are they listened to?

This approach allows you to see yourself from a third-party perspective. Then, please reflect on how your actions impact your child. I know this exercise might seem a bit strange. But trust me, when you see yourself the way your kids see you, you'll think twice before acting out.

Your kids will appreciate the effort you've made.

In the next chapter, we will seriously drill down on techniques and strategies you can use to help you manage your anger and help you focus on your children's feelings. I guarantee the next chapter will blow your mind!

[xxxi] Duraku, Z. H. (2018). Parenting Stress and its Influencing Factors Among Kosovar Mothers. *Psychology Applications & Developments III C, February*, 215-221.

[xxxii] Prikhidko, A., & Swank, J. M. (2020). Exhausted parents experience of anger: the relationship between anger and burnout. *The Family Journal, 28*(3), 283-289.

[xxxiii] Tsai, A. (2019). *Gaining control: Anger management group for adolescents* (Doctoral dissertation, California State University, Northridge).

CHAPTER 4
Keeping the Snowball atop the Hill

The greatest weapon against stress is our ability to choose one thought over another.

- WILLIAM JAMES

Once it gets rolling, it can quickly grow into a massive problem. At first, the little snowball doesn't seem like much. But once it's about halfway down, stopping can be virtually impossible.

I'm sure you've been there before. Well, we've all been there before. You think you've got everything together, but then, suddenly, that snowball gets rolling. This chapter aims to keep that snowball from rolling down. We will talk about strategies and techniques that you can use to help you keep that tiny snowball put. In particular, we'll focus on how our ability to control negative emotions is all about choice.

Yes, that's right.

Controlling anger, bitterness, resentment, and disappointment, all of these emotions depend on our choices. We can choose to embrace negative emotions. We can also choose to rid ourselves of them. Please note that we're not talking about sweeping negative emotions under the rug. We're ridding ourselves of the chain reaction leading to the snowball rolling down the hill.

Also, we'll be discussing a crucial topic: how to reconnect with your child following a fight—taking the appropriate steps to right the ship after negative interactions are essential. So, don't touch that dial because so much is coming your way!

Address It, Don't Repress It

Sadly, one of the most common misconceptions surrounding anger management is suppression. Some people believe the best way to deal with anger is not to get angry in the first place. Now, hear me out. There is some merit to that approach.

Allow me to elaborate.

If you plan to remove yourself from negative situations, that's perfectly fine. I would encourage you to do so. I recommend that you avoid problems that push all of your buttons. For instance, you and your child constantly argue over what to watch on television. So, it's best to avoid the entire situation and find a better activity.

However, this approach fails when you can't sidestep an issue. For example, you cannot avoid becoming involved in your child's schoolwork when grades are down. Yes, you know there will be fireworks. But you cannot afford to stay out of the situation. You must intervene before it's too late.

So, does suppressing emotions work in this situation?

Not quite. Attempting to sweep your frustration under the rug may lead to a needless outburst. So, it's best to handle any negative emotions proactively. First, you must address the issue. Don't hide the fact that you're upset. Instead, express why you're upset. Respect your child by telling them why you feel the way you do. There is no need to yell. You can discuss your feelings, so your child knows where you're coming from.

Next, ask your child how **they** feel. Encourage **them** to speak. If you feel a negative emotion build up, don't try to hide it. Tell your child why you don't like the conversation's direction. Ultimately, the aim is to have an honest two-way discussion where both of you have the opportunity to express your feelings without fear of losing your cool.

So, what happens if you do?

In that case, you need a timeout. Communicate it to your child. Also, tell them it's best to take a step back and resume the discussion once your feelings have subsided.

Thinking carefully about my words beforehand has helped me avoid many unpleasant moments. Thinking my words through has enabled me to say what I want without fear of losing my cool. Moreover, I build an expectation of what my children might reply to. In doing so, I try my best to avoid being surprised by an unexpected reply.

No, I know what you're thinking. This exercise is excellent when you have older kids, but what about if you have little ones?

My advice is to talk to your children about your feelings in the simplest possible terms. For instance, statements such as "mommy feel sad when you yell" can go a long way toward helping your child understand how their behavior affects your feelings. Please remember that children, no matter how young they are, will know when you're sad or upset.

The bottom line is that you must strive to communicate your feelings as much as possible. Repressing your emotions will eventually lead to an outburst you may be unable to control. So, why let feelings spill over like that? Instead, take the time to express your feelings, and have a meaningful conversation. It's always best, to be honest about how you feel. This approach builds trust and fosters close communication.

Getting a Grip on the Snowball

Expressing your feelings is a great place to start. Nevertheless, you may need some extra help in managing your negative emotions. So, I'd like to share with you some exercises that have worked wonders for me in the past.

Are you ready? Let's get on with it!

Anger management techniques

All right, you've tried your best to express your feelings. You've tried to be straightforward and transparent about your emotions. However, things simply get to you. At this point, you feel there's nothing you can do to keep the ball from rolling down the hill.

Well, let me tell you that there's plenty you can do. Here are three quick anger management exercises you can try when things get heated.

1. Go on the move

Physical exercise is a beautiful way to release tension and stress. Now, I'm not asking you to go out and run a marathon to calm down. I am asking you to get up and do any type of exercise. When in the classroom, I play some music and have the kids dance with me. There's nothing like moving your body to clear your mind. Something as simple as taking a short walk can help me regroup, calm down, and gather my thoughts. Then, I can go back and address the situation assertively.

Please don't underestimate the power of physical activity. It is a beautiful way for you to relieve negative emotions. This reason is why I always recommend doing regular exercise. You don't need to hit the gym for three hours a day. Any physical activity is enough to make a significant difference in your body and your mental health.

2. Use your imagination

I believe in the power of visualization.

Yes, that's right! Visualization is a beautiful exercise you can try whenever you want to relieve negative emotions. Best of all, you can do visualization any time, and it doesn't take more than a few minutes.

ReAction

Here's a quick and easy exercise you can try:

- First, as you feel the onset of anger, take a timeout as soon as you can·

Then, remove yourself from the negative situation. Go someplace quiet and close your eyes.

- Next, try to picture the stressful situation. Think about why it's getting to you. Most importantly, try envisioning the specific cause of your negative emotions.
- Once you have focused on the cause of your emotions, let your imagination run free for a bit. Picture how you could solve the issue. I call this the "magic wand." Imagine you have a magic wand, so try to use it to solve the problem magically.
- Lastly, open your eyes, take a couple of deep breaths, and regroup.

I am aware that there is no magic wand. After all, serious issues don't magically disappear. However, there is a method to the madness. You see, when we let our minds free, we open ourselves to potential solutions. In particular, we tend to get caught up in our emotions. We feel that there is no way out. When we unshackle our minds, we can give ourselves the freedom to explore possibilities. This point is where that wonderful Aha! Moments happen.

Now, here is another application for this exercise. Whenever possible, use this technique to reflect on stressful situations you've had. For example, use this visualization technique to dissect an unpleasant encounter you had with your child earlier this morning or last week. Try to relive the incident focusing on what you could have done better. In doing so, you can spot possible ways to improve how you handle things for next time.

Visualization is also great when you have a subject to approach. For instance, you can visualize how a conversation with your child might go. You can anticipate your child's responses and reactions while planning yours. This approach will allow you to have a game plan, reducing your chances of losing your temper. While doing so, remember our discussion from the last chapter. Use your empathy and remember to put yourself in your child's place.

I would encourage you to try this visualization technique right away. I guarantee you'll find it helpful to anticipate your responses and, most importantly, keep that snowball atop the hill.

3. Muscle relaxation

Tension can build up almost instantly in your body when you get upset. I've found that my arms and shoulders feel sore after I've been outraged.

Why is that?

When we get upset, our muscles tend to get tense. This response is due to the fight-or-flight response in our brains. As a result, our brains are hardwired to react forcefully to stress. As you know, stress is a powerful force. Nevertheless, stress was not necessarily meant to be a bad thing. Stress was meant to be part of our survival mechanism.

ReAction

Allow me to digress for a moment.

Our ancestors used stress to identify dangerous situations. Think of humans thousands of years ago. They needed a physical response to trigger survival mechanisms. As a result, stress became an essential tool our ancestors used to spot danger and react to it accordingly.

Now, fast forward thousands of years later. We're no longer running for our lives all day long. We live relatively quiet and peaceful lives. However, the stress response is still there. So, when we get upset, we jump into that survival mode our ancestors developed. Our muscles tighten, our pulse rate climbs, and we start breathing heavily. Overexposure to this response can take its toll on your body.

What can we do about it, then?

Muscle relaxation is the answer!

This technique is brilliant in its simplicity. You can do it while in a stressful situation or try it once things have settled down. You can even teach your kids to do it with you!

Here's how it works:

- First, find a comfortable place to sit or lie down.
- Next, take a couple of deep breaths. Breathe in, clench your muscles (hands, arms, legs, shoulders), hold for a count of three, and then relax your muscles as you exhale.
- Then, shake your arms and legs. Rotate your shoulders. Open and close your hands. Move your body as much

as you can while you inhale through the nose and exhale with a sigh.

- Lastly, stretch your arms and legs as much as possible.

Don't worry if you can't sit or lie down. You can do this exercise standing up while in the hallway, in the bathroom, or at your desk. You can do it anywhere. I've done it on the bus! Plus, it doesn't take long. You only need a couple of minutes to help you build up tension and release it. Trust me. Once you get the hang of this exercise, you'll be doing it all the time.

Keeping the Snowball from Running Over Your Kids

When that snowball gets rolling, there may be no way of stopping it. Along the way, it might run over your kids. If that's the case, the consequence may be tough to handle. As such, it's crucial to build an action plan to help you manage your negative emotions when dealing with your children.

So, I've developed this ten-step plan to help you manage your negative emotions when dealing with your children. It's worked for me, so I'm sure it'll work for you. I'd like to share it with you.

1. Set boundaries and expectations.

One of the most significant issues I see is the lack of clear boundaries. Think about that for a minute. We have expectations about how our children should behave, but do we communicate these expectations to them? Do these expectations meet reality?

Similarly, we have boundaries. There are certain limits that we do not allow our children to cross. If they do, we tend to scold or punish them. However, do our kids know what those boundaries are?

It's not fair to just assume they know. Boundaries and expectations should be set in advance. It's not enough to tell your children once. We must lead by example and model how we expect them to behave. It is also crucial to remind them over and over about where the limits are, especially for the little ones. In doing so, children know where they stand. Please remember that children need structure. They crave it. Having rules, limits, and routines help children feel safe. Your child will feel secure knowing you are there for them.

So, the first significant step is to communicate your limits and expectations. There's no need for a big sermon. Consider this example:

Your children spend way too much time on their phones. Instead of scolding them about it, schedule a time of the day when they are allowed to use them. Inform your children about the dangers of too much screen time. Then, use positive reinforcement, such as joint playtime. If they resist, communicate your feelings. Let them know that you're concerned for their wellbeing. Your attitude is the result of your concern for their wellbeing. Speaking from the heart is always the best policy.

2. Avoid acting out in anger.

In other words, do nothing! Your new default setting ought to be doing nothing when angry. Yes, I know that might seem counterintuitive, but hear me out. When we're mad, we tend to lose control over our actions. We seemingly let our emotions get the best of us. That's why we say and do things that we later regret. So, the next step is simple. Please don't do anything when you feel angry or upset. Take a time out and cool down. You can always decide what to do later.

3. Listen instead of talking.

I know this next step is going to be pretty tough to handle. During an argument, our instinct is to start talking over the other person. That may be fine in the boardroom, but with your child, it will not cut it. I beg of you to take the time to listen. Really listen. Whatever happens, please stop talking and let your child speak. Let them express their feelings confidently. They need to know that even when you're angry, you're there for them. Otherwise, they will fear your wrath. Naturally, that is not a good place to be. So, please avoid acting out in anger and listen instead of talking. You'll be so glad you did.

4. Avoid escalation.

All right, anger bounces off others and lands back in your lap. Think of it like a giant rubber ball. The harder you toss it, the harder it will return to you. Your child will react accordingly when you engage your child in a fight. As such, this is not a good state. Consider this:

- Your toddler throws himself on the floor. So, you lash out at them by raising your voice. The child almost immediately bursts into tears. Their crying annoys you even more. You keep yelling, and the child is crying louder. Do you see the escalation here?
- Your teen doesn't clean their room. You lose your cool and rip into them. Your teen doesn't hold back and starts yelling back. All of a sudden, you're now in a yelling match. Do you see the escalation here?
- In both situations, anger might be inevitable. Nevertheless, your reaction is. So, the best policy is to avoid escalation. Take a step back. There is no need to fear your child won't respect you. If anything, they will respect you more for being mature enough to know when to pull away. Once tempers have cooled down, you can listen instead of talking.

5. Be careful with threats.

A threat is a potent tool. Threats are highly effective on one condition: you must follow through on them. If you fail to follow through, your children will quickly see that you're bluffing. They will call your bluff eventually. When that occurs, you have no choice but to up the ante.

Consider this situation:

Your children are running around the house with a ball. You have told them repeatedly to stop horsing around and take the ball out because someone might get hurt. Your warnings fall on deaf ears. So, you threaten your children: "I'm going to take the ball away! I will take it in 1...2...3..."

There are two paths at this point:

- First, you follow through on your threat. The kids won't settle down, so you take the ball away. They can kick and scream all they want, but it won't make you budge unless they get their act together.
- Second, you don't follow through. The kids call your bluff, and you back down. You will continue running after them, begging them to stop. Now the kids know they're the ones who are in charge.

I know this scenario may seem funny on the surface, but let's admit it happens all the time. You see, many parents fear hurting their children. These parents are afraid that if they withhold from their kids, they may cause harm to them.

It's OK to feel that way. This reason is what we are here for. But please remember that your job is to create conditions for your children to grow healthy. It's your job because you love them. No one needs to tell you to do it. It's in your DNA.

So, I would suggest you use threats sparingly but effectively. Let your kids know you're in charge. It's for their own good. They know you see them. You're the boss, not because you're domineering, but because you want to take care of them. It's in your blood to protect them.

6. It's not what you say. It's how you say it.

Your tone of voice, pitch, and intonation all signal something. Do you recall when your mom or dad had "that tone" in their voice? You knew you were in trouble whenever you heard your parents' voice change. Well, it ought to be the same with you. However, there is a catch.

A stern tone of voice is perfectly fine when dealing with a serious matter. Your kids know you are serious, so they must pay attention. The catch lies in using a mocking or hurtful tone. Consider these examples:

- Your child didn't pick up their toys. You've told them to do it thousands of times. Out of frustration, you say, *"what's wrong with you?"* A sarcastic tone accompanied by these words can be enough to send a child up the wall. Your comments and tone imply that the child is unintelligent. Needless to say, this is a hurtful expression.

In contrast, using a sing-song tone will not cut it when you're serious. Your child needs to differentiate between when you're serious and when you're playing around. Choose an assertive yet respectful tone when approaching serious matters. Above all, consistency is the name of the game. Children respond to structure. Consistency is an enormous part of a healthy structure.

7. Take your time to discipline

Discipline comes in many ways. You can remove privileges or restrict certain liberties. However, the worst kind of discipline comes when you're angry. For example, yelling at your child when you're mad is not discipline. It's just a lousy way of venting your frustration.

Please note that I am not asking you to forget about discipline. What I am asking you to do is to avoid punishment when you're angry. Instead, let your child know that their actions will have consequences. But instead of quickly sorting out the issue, you need to calm down first. The best part of this approach is that your child will see that you're fair. Your child can't blame you for overreaction because you have taken the time to cool down, listen to them, and then hand out discipline accordingly.

8. Physical force is a big no-no!

A grave misconception is that discipline involves some type of physical punishment. Punishments like spanking may have the opposite effect on your child's psyche. A 2008 study found that "There is substantial research evidence that physical punishment makes it more, not less, likely that children will be defiant and aggressive in the future."

So, what does this research tell us?

It's screaming, at the top of its lungs, that physical punishment is not the answer. If anything, physical punishment has the opposite effect on your child. Over time, exposure to physical punishment breeds violence in your child.

From now on, I want to beg you to avoid any physical punishment. Instead, talk to your child. Try your best to reason with them. Take all the time you need to regroup. Find more productive ways of disciplining your child. As they grow, you won't need to "punish" them. Quite the contrary, your child will learn to understand their mistakes. The best-case scenario is to foster a sense of accountability in your children. That way, when they make a mistake, they will own up to it. That effect precludes the need for punishment.

9. Discuss healthy ways to cope with anger

Leading by example is a great way to guide your children. As such, discussing healthy ways to cope with anger is a must. Your children must see that you're able to handle your anger healthily.

When discussing coping strategies with your children, list acceptable ways to handle anger. For instance:

- Tell others about your feelings without attacking them.
- Sing or dance around when you're feeling frustrated.
- If you feel like hitting someone, kick a ball outside.
- Let others know you're angry and you need a breath of fresh air.

Discussing coping strategies helps your children see there is nothing wrong with getting angry. The issue lies in not knowing how to handle it. Together, you can work out practical ways of expressing your anger without escalating the conflict or hurting others. Have an open discussion with your kids about what helps them calm down and what they feel might also help them.

10. Know when to walk away

Lastly, please remember there is no shame in walking away. Often, we feel like we shouldn't back down from a confrontation. That may be true if you're defending your child from danger. But when you're engaging with your child, it's best to avoid unnecessary conflict.

I would like to encourage you to walk away from conflict, especially if you feel you might lose control. You can always take a time out, take a deep breath, focus, and regroup. Once you've regrouped, you can address the situation more effectively.

At the end of the day, thinking things through is always better than getting caught up in the heat of the moment. Believe me. You'll be glad that you took an extra moment, or two, to think about your response and decisions.

After the Snowball

So, what happens if you can't stop the snowball? When the snowball rolls down the hill, and you just can't stop it in time.

Yes, you know what I mean. What happens when it seems too late to stop a confrontation? In some instances, it might be a minor rift. In others, it might be a major argument. Regardless of the confrontation's scale, it's an unfortunate incident. Left unattended, the underlying feelings can fester, leading to even worse conflicts. So, we must do something about it.

But what?

The answer is reconnecting with your child.

I have an eight-step plan I'd like to share with you. This plan has worked for me, and I'm sure it will work for you. This plan lays out how you can reconnect with your child even after the worst confrontation.

Spoiler alert: this plan focuses on communication!

1. Take a step back

All right, so it's happened. The snowball had rolled, and there was nothing you could do to stop it. Once you realize the snowball is out of control, removing yourself from the situation is the best action. The last thing you want to do is escalate the confrontation. Getting into a shouting match is not going to do you any favors.

So, what can you do?

Physically extricate yourself from the situation. Go into another room. Get a glass of water. Allow your child to go to their room and cool down. You can always take the time to regroup and address the issue in a calmer state of mind.

2. Apologize

Apologizing does not demean your parenting position. If anything, it shows your child that you're willing to recognize when you've made a mistake. Apologize for things such as raising your voice, letting the situation get out of control, or losing your temper. Please remember that you are the adult. So, it's essential to show that you understand what's happened and the importance of rectifying the situation.

3. Bridge the gap

Bridging the gap means approaching your child first. Don't wait for them to come to you. After all, your child may be afraid to approach you, especially if they fear your reaction. Show then that you don't hold any grudges. Your love for them is much greater than any argument. Give them a minute if your child is not ready to talk to you. They will surely come around soon enough. Then, you can reestablish communication.

4. Discuss the causes

Once you've reestablished communication, it's crucial to discuss what happened. Take the opportunity to explore the grounds of the argument. Above all, it's critical to avoid assigning blame. The last thing you want is to blame your child or anyone else, for that matter. If there are mistakes, it's best to own up to them and address them openly. If that means you made a mistake, then own up to it, and find the best solution.

5. Explain your side of the issue

It's vital that you explain your side of the problem. Your child needs to know how you feel. Take the time to explain your reaction. Rationalize it so your child sees that they are not the cause of the argument. Tell them you're upset about their behavior if you reacted to something they did. Above all, reassure your child. Tell them that you love them even if you don't like their behavior.

6. Ask for your child's opinion.

Now, here's a critical step: give your child a chance to explain their side of the story. But please listen! Listen to their feelings, opinions, and perception. Give them the freedom to speak. You may not like what they have to say. But the important thing is to ensure you have bridged the gap.

Once you have both sides of the story, it's time to find a solution. Whatever the situation, always strive to meet your child halfway. This approach may also mean that you'll have to make changes.

Please look at it this way:

An argument is an excellent opportunity to set a "before and after" in your relationship. You can make changes to address issues that require attention. This opportunity could be the best time to right the ship and sail in a new direction.

7. Turn the page

Turning the page is a critical part of reconnecting. Once the confrontation is over, you've discussed the issue, proposed a solution, and moved on. Go out and do something fun. Anything! Watch a movie. Play games. Schedule some family fun time—Cook a yummy dinner. Anything goes here. The point is to focus on the "after" part. The "before" is in the past. That past is something you want to forget gradually. Now, it's time to focus on spending quality time.

8. Talk to a trusted source

On the surface, the issue may seem solved. However, confrontations can be emotionally charged situations. As a result, there may be feelings lingering beneath the surface. If so, talking to a trusted source such as a close friend, counselor, or spiritual advisor can help you and your child find closure. Often, a third-party perspective can help you ground your thoughts and recalibrate your parenting scope.

Lastly, please remember that we all go through rough patches. You and your child are not immune to it. There will be times when things get out of hand. So, it's best to have a trusted plan you can rely on when needed. Please take the time to establish open communication with your child. Your child needs to know they can come to you whenever necessary. Opening your mind and heart is the best way to ensure your child's feelings flow naturally instead of gushing out like Old Faithful.

A Key Reflection

I'm sure you've felt overwhelmed at times. Indeed, it's not easy being a parent. There are so many moving parts to effective parenting. When you think about it, being a mother is one of the most complex and demanding jobs out there. But we do it with all of our hearts because we love our kids. There is no amount of money in the world that could compensate for the love we have for our kids.

But sometimes you don't feel good enough, like, you're not up to the task. Have you ever felt this way? Don't be ashamed to admit it. I've been there before.

There is a psychological phenomenon known as the "imposter syndrome." This phenomenon boils down to our perception of what everyone else does around us. For instance, you see other moms that seem to have it all together. They make life, work, and parenting seem easy. It's like they get out of bed, and everything goes their way.

In the meantime, you feel completely lost at times. You feel like you don't have a clue what you're doing. Don't worry if you've ever felt like this. Trust me. We've all been there at one point or another.

ReAction

So, what can we do about this imposter syndrome?

First of all, please give yourself a break. You don't need to be perfect. No one is. Give yourself credit where credit is due. Please avoid dwelling on the mistakes you've made. Those are in the past. The present and future are within your control. The time has come for you to control what's in your hands. You have everything you need to make your children's lives the best they can be.

So, the next time you feel like an "imposter," like someone who doesn't deserve any credit, think about all the beautiful things you've already achieved. I guarantee that someone out there looks at you and feels you're the parent of the year!

You don't believe me... I promise you that plenty of people out there wish they could be in your position.

I'd like to close this chapter by asking you to reflect on your life. Express gratitude for all the good things you've got going on. Make an effort to list all the things you're thankful for. This list will help us link the next part of our discussion. In the next chapter, we'll be focusing on you!

So, stay tuned. There's a lot more to come!

CHAPTER 5
Putting Yourself First

If your compassion does not include yourself, it is incomplete.

- JACK KORNFIELD

I know what you're thinking. Easier said than done. If anything, you are putting everyone else ahead of you. I get that. However, there comes a time when we need to think about ourselves. We need to focus on taking care of ourselves. It took me a while to get it, but I realized how important self-care truly is when I did.

Here is the rationale:

You can't expect to take care of others and be the pillar in your home if you're not well. You can't bring your A-game if you're tired, sick, and burned out. Taking the time to renew and recharge your energies is crucial in ensuring your success as a parent, professional, friend, and partner.

In this chapter, you are going to put yourself first! We will discover self-care as a great way of preventing conflict in your relationships and creating a safe and predictable environment for your child. Also, we'll be taking actionable steps to ensure that you manage your working, family, and personal time so that you can avoid anger and frustration altogether.

Does that sound too good to be true?

I can assure you it's not!

Taking Care of Your Needs

As parents, we generally view putting ourselves first as a selfish attitude. While it's natural to feel that way, please remember that you can't pour from an empty cup. You know how you must put on your oxygen mask before helping others with theirs on a flight?

After all, how can you be there for others if you're not doing well?

Think about it for a minute.

For most of us, life means working late, getting little sleep, forgetting about weekends, and having practically zero personal time.

But it shouldn't be that way.

You see, we can keep up this pace for a while. We can put our heads down and power through. But there comes a time when it's simply too much. We need a break. We need to take our foot off the gas and recover. I know that's hard to do. It took me a while to see the importance of self-care.

How important is self-care?

Taking care of yourself is vital to ensure you always bring your best. So, allow me to discuss Maslow's Hierarchy of Needs. This prevalent theory explains what needs we must fulfill to reach our peak performance.

Allow me to discuss Maslow's Hierarchy of Needs.

Abraham Maslow was a psychologist whose research yielded five levels of human needs. Each group represents things that we need in our lives to be happy and fulfilled. [xxxiv]

Here is a breakdown of each level: [xxxv]

1. Physiological needs

This level is the basic one. Here, we're talking about survival. As a result, we're not exactly focused on being happy. We're merely trying to stay alive. Situations such as food, shelter, and sleep are the main goals of this level.

2. Safety needs

By "safety," we're talking about preserving our physical integrity beyond purely physiological needs. We're focused on surviving once we have fulfilled our necessities. We focus on security, health, and employment at this level.

3. Love and belonging

The third level focuses more on emotional and psychological needs. We're talking about friendship, family, intimacy, and connection. We focus on being part of a family and a community.

4. *Esteem*

This level focuses specifically on how we perceive ourselves. Thus, we're talking about self-esteem, status, respect, recognition, and freedom. Current interpretations of this level also extend to the broader family context, not just the individual.

5. *Self-actualization*

This level is the highest. It focuses on realizing our true potential. Once we have covered all our basic needs, we can move on to developing our potential into the reality that we envision for our lives.

Most people in first-world countries don't really need to worry about food, shelter, and personal security. While people in developing countries must toil to meet these needs, folks in first-world nations can assume their basic needs are met. These basic needs correspond to the first two levels.

When our basic needs are met, we can focus on levels three through five. In particular, our discussion focuses on the third and fourth levels.

Think about it for a minute.

You strive to cement your role within your family and community. Throughout this book, we've discussed the importance of bolstering the connection with your child. Please remember that we're talking about building a sense of belonging. In other words, fostering a sense of unity with your child is essential. It's about helping your child see that you're one family unit. Of course, there is room for individuality. But at the end of the day, you're one family.

I'd also like to point out how vital self-esteem is. We often overlook self-esteem because we're too busy getting the job done. We're always on the go, taking care of kids, work, and life. So, it's common to forego nurturing our self-esteem and self-respect. When your self-esteem and self-respect become neglected, your energy and drive can take a hit.

How so?

You see, low self-esteem tends to be a predictor of anxiety and depression. In turn, depression gnaws at your self-esteem.[xxxvi] This negative relationship breeds a vicious cycle. Low self-esteem fosters anxiety and depression, while increased anxiety and depression further fuel low self-esteem.

This trap is one we must avoid at all costs.

We must strive to boost our self-esteem as much as possible. We cannot afford to let stress and anxiety get in the way of building a positive relationship within ourselves. This reason underscores my argument. I am urging you at this time to take your self-esteem and self-respect needs seriously. I know that it's your nature to put yourself last. But I am pleading with you here. You must make time for yourself. This time doesn't mean dropping everything and forgetting the world exists. What I am suggesting is that you take as much as possible. Even a few minutes daily allows you to disconnect from the world and recharge.

It doesn't take much to find this disconnect and recharge. Sometimes, all it takes is a warm bath, a vigorous exercise session, or curling up with a good book. The main idea is to give yourself a breather. After all, it's virtually impossible to be "on" all the time, no matter how hard you try.

As for self-actualization, please remember that the highest level is possible through fulfilling your goals and dreams. Let me tell you that being a great parent is part and parcel of self-actualization. Here's how it works. Being a great parent is one of people's most cherished dreams. Who doesn't dream of seeing their children grow up to become happy and prosperous?

Of course! We all dream of a bright future for our children. We may not be sure what that future will look like, but we're all hoping for the best. A common misconception is that self-actualization is about realizing your dreams. While that is true, realizing your dreams also involves seeing your children reach their full potential. Ultimately, being a great parent is a way that we can achieve the highest level of Maslow's hierarchy.

At this point, I'd like to underscore one more thing. We all need time to take a break. Trying hard to be "on" 24/7 can eventually lead to burnout. Now, it's true that some folks can handle more than others. But that's not the point. Regardless of how much you can take, the fact is that you need to prioritize yourself. In doing so, you can always be at your best game. You owe it to yourself.

How to Disconnect and Reconnect

It's hard being "on" all the time. We try so hard to, but there comes a time when we need to pull the plug and reset. Being "on" all the time not only leads to burnout but also takes away from quality time with our family.

When you disconnect, you have a golden opportunity to reconnect with your loved ones. In today's uber-busy world, we must prioritize reconnecting with our partners, kids, and friends. We can't afford to let everything else get the best of us.

Author and motivational speaker Regina Brett once said:

> *Sometimes, you have to disconnect to stay connected. Remember the old days when you had eye contact during a conversation? When everyone wasn't looking down at a device in their hands? We've become so focused on that tiny screen that we forget the big picture, the people right in front of us.*

Wow! That's all I can say.

Regina makes a clear point about technology. And yes, it's true. We're all too caught up in our phones, tablets, and computers. But our fixation on individual issues makes it hard for us to connect at a genuinely personal level.

Let's take a moment to ponder that thought.

When was the last time you had a heartfelt conversation with your kids? Your partner? Your friends? We get so tied up with work, school, soccer practice, bake sales, and church that we neglect ourselves.

The time has come for it to end. The time has come to move away from our reliance on technology and obsessing about the little things. The time has come to disconnect and reconnect. I would like you to forget about anything getting in between you and your child. Forget the arguments and the screens (also, forget about the arguments over screens). The time has come for you to unplug from negativity.

So, here's a plan I'd like to share with you. It's called a "mothering" plan. This plan intends to help you manage your schedule to devote more time to your family and less time to chores. If that sounds too good to be true, I can assure you it is not!

Let's get started with your customized mothering plan right now!

Mothering your time

Let's begin devising your plan to 'mother your time' by defining what the plan means. In short, your mothering time means setting yourself up for success. Have you ever heard the expression, "when you fail to plan, you plan to fail?" That's precisely what I'm getting at here. Your personalized mothering plan is about putting yourself in a position to be successful. You can achieve this outcome by carefully planning your day every day.

Trust me. You don't need to become a control freak. All you need to do is put some thought into your daily activities. So, let's get on with your new step-by-step mothering plan.

Set yourself up for success

All right, we've talked about why you need to set yourself up for success. It's essential to plan your days so you can avoid the worst parts of your usual day-to-day routine.

What do I mean by that?

The constant churning that comes with always running from one activity to the next. You feel like you never have enough time for anything. By the end of the day, you're beaten, frustrated, and grumpy, and your energy levels zapped to nothing.

Now, picture this:

Your home is tidy. Your inbox is free and clear. You have plenty of time to play with your kids and enough time to take a relaxing bath.

Does that sound too good to be true?

I can assure you it's not!

I've done it. I do it all the time.

Does that mean I have a special trick up my sleeve?

No. I have the power of planning at my disposal.

You see, planning your day as detailed as possible helps you manage the multitude of tasks you handle daily. I don't mean carrying a stopwatch around with you all the time. I mean, focusing on what you have to do and the time you realistically have to complete it.

For instance, knowing what tasks you need to complete daily can help you focus on what needs to be done. Doing so can clear much of the useless clutter that clogs up your day. When you plan your days, you realize you lose precious time on meaningless tasks.

What do I mean by "meaningless?" Worrying about things you can't control, such as traffic jams. But if you plan, a traffic jam won't derail your day.

So, how can you set yourself up for success?

Here is my four-step plan that will help you get on the right track:

1. First, divide your day up into time boxes. Each box can be one or a half hour or a full hour. I recommend breaking up your day into half-hour chunks. After all, not every activity will take you an hour to complete. Please allocate your time boxes to your various activities, such as dropping kids off at school, work, chores, sleep, etc. You can also block off time for activities such as going out with your family or having lunch with friends. You can even block off an entire day if you need to!

2. Next, fill up some time boxes for self-care activities. You don't need to block off hours on end. Even one thirty-minute slot for meditation, yoga, or taking a nap can go a long way toward helping you stay focused.

3. Then, make sure you don't miss important stuff. Please ensure you've allocated time for chores such as laundry, paying bills, running errands, and cooking. Realistically,

it's impossible to get everything done all the time. So, you need to prioritize. I strongly suggest moving the most important things to the front line. For instance, paying bills and grocery shopping are two tasks you should get done asap.

4. Lastly, plan your time for the fun stuff. This time ought to be devoted to playing with your kids, snuggling, reading stories, running around in the backyard, going to the park, you name it. Also, don't be afraid to use this time for yourself. Use it for hobbies, watching your favorite TV show, or just getting a glass of wine and unwinding.

Please remember that planning takes some time and practice. Once you get the hang of it, it'll be easy. You won't need to struggle to keep up. You'll feel increasingly in control of everything that happens around you.

Here are a couple of pro tips I'd like to share with you:

1. Quit multitasking!

You might think that you get more done when juggling various issues simultaneously. However, I can assure you that's not the case. An interesting 2012 study concluded that multitasking was efficient based on how you measure it. Multitaskers appear to be more productive when you estimate how much they get done. Multitaskers, in contrast, show declining performance when measured in terms of accuracy.

So, what does this mean?

We believe we perform better because we seem to get more things done. However, being busier doesn't necessarily mean we're doing something to the best of our capabilities.

In conclusion, stop multitasking if you want to do things as best you can. Focusing on individual tasks, and getting them done as quickly as possible, is better than trying to do everything at once. Unfortunately, many things slip through the cracks when you have a penchant for multitasking..[xxxvii]

2. When in doubt, delegate!

I know what you're thinking, "there is so much I have to do. I can't just drop everything and focus on a single task at a time." Well, I'm here to tell you that you can do just that. I would encourage you to delegate as many tasks as you can. You see, delegating is about getting others to take things off your plate. Also, using automation is a great way to relieve yourself of unnecessary stress.

Consider this situation:

You can automate bill payments, so you don't have to think about them. This simple tweak can help free up precious time and attention so that you can get other tasks done. Please remember that minutes at a time add up. Before you know it, you'll have extra hours on hand.

Can you get a housekeeper? I get it. Most people can't afford a full-time housekeeper. But could you hire someone for a few hours a week? You see, these small changes add up. If there's anything you can get someone else to do for you, do it! The time and effort you free up are much better spent on yourself and your kids.

3. Less is more!

Clutter is one of the things that tie us down so much. I mean, think about it—clothes, toys, gadgets, shoes... everywhere. We often run after everything trying to keep our home organized. Well, I'm here to tell you that less is more.

In short, the less stuff you have, the better off you are. Downsizing into a bit of a minimalist style helps you free up valuable space. Perhaps there's stuff you can just put way into storage. The point is to keep the essentials on hand. Doing so means less stuff to clean up and less clutter to worry about. Here are three principles that I live by:

- Have a place for everything. Designate a home for every item. Over time, keys, phones, books, clothes, everything will automatically be put back in their place. Designating specific locations for everything makes the organization much more manageable.
- Clear surfaces. Having neat surfaces not only looks good but also saves on needless distractions.
- Embrace empty spaces. Don't be afraid to have open spaces or corners. Not having anything in a spot means something less to worry about. Do you know what that means? More time and focus on other things like you and your kids.

I would highly encourage you to give your mothering plan a try. Take out a notebook, laptop, or notetaking app on your phone.

Make your plan. Commit to it. Try it out for a month. As you go along, make as many tweaks as you need. You'll see that you'll never go back after a couple of weeks!

Getting a Grip on Sleep

Sleep is one of the first things to go out the window when you become a parent. Do you recall those first few days with a new baby? Oh yes... lots of short nights. Of course, sleep does get better as children get older. Nevertheless, the number of activities in your life may not allow you to get as much sleep as you need.

Remember that sleep is key for helping you stay on top of your game.

How so?

Sleep deprivation is a serious issue. I'm not talking about a couple of nights of short sleep. I'm talking about prolonged exposure to lack of sleep. This phenomenon is called "sleep deprivation" and can seriously affect your overall quality of life.

A 2010 study revealed that sleep deprivation significantly affects cognitive ability. In other words, lack of sleep adversely affects our ability to process information, stay alert, and think clearly.[xxxviii]

No surprise, right?

Well, you might be surprised to find that cognitive decline impacts our ability to process emotions. Since our mental abilities diminish the less we sleep, our ability to process emotional stimuli also becomes considerably weaker.

So, what does this mean?

Not getting enough sleep dramatically reduces our ability to process emotions. In particular, our tolerance for certain situations makes it quite challenging to manage our feelings appropriately. These findings explain why not resting enough causes moodiness and irritability.

A fascinating 2014 study looked into how sleep deprivation affects people's ability to empathize with others. Unsurprisingly, the sleep-deprived test subjects showed lower levels of empathy than the control subjects. These results demonstrate how sleep deprivation reduces our tolerance of others, that is, our capacity to display empathy.

So, how does this study tie into our discussion?

Think about it this way. When we're rested, we have a much higher tolerance for others. In contrast, we generally have little patience for others when we're on no sleep. This condition explains why it's so hard to manage certain situations at home following short nights.

Based on this evidence, I urge you to make sleep a priority. I know that getting a whole night's sleep isn't always possible. I get that some nights you just can't get to bed early. There are other days when you have to get up early.

I get it. I've been there.

Because I've been there, I urge you to make time for sleep. Getting as much sleep as possible is the best way to improve your overall quality of life. Most importantly, getting enough sleep improves your overall health and wellness.

Why do you think professional athletes have a strict sleeping regimen?

Coaches know that athletes must rest to recover from stress.

Stress?

You see, professional athletes undergo a significant amount of physical, emotional, and psychological stress. Therefore, they need sleep to recover from these stressors. When athletes don't get enough rest, they don't have a chance to recover. Ultimately, this lack of recovery can lead to injuries..[xxxix]

If we translate this concept into our lives, we can see that sleep is necessary to recover from the stress we deal with every day. Without sleep, your body cannot function properly. Your mind and body don't have the chance to disconnect and repair damage caused by our usual wear and tear.

So, how can you improve your sleep?

There's a trick the military uses to get more sleep. Sleep whenever you can. Yes, that's right. You must sleep whenever you can. If you can't get eight hours of sleep every night, make as much time as possible to sleep. It doesn't matter how or where you get it. The point is to get it.

I am a huge fan of power naps. Taking short naps, say 15 or 20 minutes, can give you a boost to last two or three hours. Also, taking longer naps, say about an hour, can help you get through a tough afternoon, especially when you're on short rest.

Above all, I would encourage you to experiment until you find your best approach. Some folks like to take two or three mini-naps throughout the day. Others prefer to take one longer nap, say at midday or mid-afternoon. Others would like to go to bed early to get an early jump on the day. Ultimately, your body will dictate what works best for you. So, don't be afraid to experiment until you find the right approach for your needs.

About Partners and Relationships

Any parent will tell you that having kids can take its toll on a relationship. However, maintaining a solid relationship is a cornerstone of healthy home life for any child. You kids need to feel safe and comfortable in their current environment. Fostering a great relationship with your spouse or partner is a great step toward creating a healthy environment for your kids.

I know it's hard to maintain a rock-solid relationship when it gets tough.

But that needs to change.

Renowned motivational speaker Tony Robbins once said, "Do what you did at the beginning of a relationship, and there won't be an end." I love this phrase because it calls us to keep the flame burning. I know that can be pretty difficult when life wallops you with so much. But it's your relationship that will keep you afloat.

This reason is why I don't believe in using "me" time to dedicate to your partner. The time you devote to your partner ought to be mutually beneficial. In other words, your time together should be about things you enjoy doing together. This situation isn't about doing something to please your spouse. This situation is about reconnecting like you did when you first met.

Do you recall those first few moments?

Generally speaking, it's common interests that bring couples together. From there, common elements help relationships grow. Of course, there are differences. But those differences aren't significant enough to split up a couple. So, the relationship grows and turns into a committed one.

The tricky part is losing sight of that magic spell.

We cannot afford to let that happen.

We must strive to keep our relationship as healthy as possible. There are two main reasons for this thought.

First, your mental and emotional health hinge on your relationship. If you're in a happy and functional relationship, your overall outlook on life will be much better. Your relationship will be one less thing to cause you stress. In contrast, a dysfunctional relationship will only add fuel to your life's stresses.

Second, a positive relationship with your partner will positively influence your children. When kids see their parents working like a well-oiled machine, they have something they can hold onto. Kids feel safe knowing their parents are in it for the long haul. Conversely, kids that see a dysfunctional relationship with their parents grow up feeling insecure.

How so?

Think about this: kids don't have a firm foundation if parents are constantly bickering and fighting (heaven forbid an abusive relationship!). Moreover, kids might feel like their parents might leave them. Living with that uncertainty can lead to serious emotional issues in children.

So, the answer here is to work on your relationship constantly. Try to make your best effort to put in as much work today as you did before. Make time for your relationship. Small things like a date night once a month can go a long way toward helping you keep the fire burning.

Here are six crucial points on which I'd like you to focus your relationship. Believe me, working on these points will boost your relationship even if everything is going great. As a result, you'll get the boost you need to up your parenting game.

1. Relationships change

Naturally, relationships change with parenthood. Being a mother brings about new responsibilities you didn't have before. Often, communication issues happen. It seems like you disagree a lot more often than you did. But don't worry about it. That's part and parcel of parenthood.

The antidote is open communication. Talking about feelings is critical. Most importantly, talking about how you feel about changes will help you work out everything. You may find that righting the ship is much easier than you think!

2. Listening to one another

Open communication is predicated on listening. I know that your partner may not always listen. So, this is something you need to keep working on. Scheduling one-on-one time is a great way to foster open communication. In particular, ask open-ended questions such as, "how do you feel about that?" Or "what do you think we can do about it?" They may seem small but can go a long way toward making an enormous difference. Above all, paying attention is key *to making open communication truly work.*

3. Talking about your feelings

Here is the hard part. Talking about your feelings may not be the easiest thing for your partner. I encourage you to avoid using "you" in the conversation. "You" statements may seem accusatory. Instead of saying, "you don't listen to me," it's best to restate it as "I feel disappointed when my opinion is not heard."

4. Accepting changes

There are certain things you simply have to accept. For instance, you may face that you won't have as much time for one another as you once did. So, embracing the change doesn't mean giving up. It means that you need to make the most of your time together. Please remember that quality is always better than quantity.

I would encourage you to make a list of changes you're prepared to accept and how to make the most of them. If there's something that you change (for instance, one of you may be able to cut back on hours at work), then it's essential to explore your options together. One-sided decisions seldom work out well.

5. Managing conflict

Let's take a time out here. Pull the plug whenever there's conflict. There's no point in keeping an argument going. Take a time out, regroup and calmly address the elephant in the room. Above all, strive to resolve the conflict. If you feel that you cannot find an adequate solution, you may want to enlist some third-party help from a counselor or spiritual advisor. Sometimes, a fresh pair of eyes can help you see things you may have missed entirely.

6. Stay connected

When things get tough, try your best to stay connected. While weekend getaways are lovely, they're not always possible. So, here is a list of things you can do to give your relationship the jumpstart it needs:

- Go to dinner or a movie. Get away for a couple of hours. Perhaps grandma and grandpa can help out for a couple of hours. Hiring a babysitter can also help take the burden off your mind.
- Take a time out at home. Watch a movie, get a glass of wine, or turn everything off and talk. You can schedule an hour or two after the kids have gone to bed.

- Reconnect with things you liked to do before you became a parent. Go back to these activities. You may not be able to devote as much time as you'd like, but you've got to start somewhere.

One last thing: please remember that your sexual relationship may have had a significant impact. But don't worry. Things eventually get back on track. However, things may not magically get back on course. You both need to talk about your feelings and expectations. I am sure you're both thinking about the same thing. So, making things work out may not be nearly as challenging as you think.

One Last Thought

A positive, stable environment is the cornerstone for your child's development. While it's essential for you to manage your schedule effectively, it's also vital for you to create a safe and predictable environment for your child. Structure, such as routines and schedules, can go a long way toward providing your child with a safety net. Children thrive when they feel safe and listened to. You can achieve that goal by providing a predictable environment that suits their needs.

In addition, I'd like to offer you advice:

Ask your child about their feelings. Ask them how they feel about life around them. If you ask them, they will tell you. Your child's point of view is a critical component in ensuring that your mothering time plan works perfectly.

I know it might not be a conversation to have when your child is relatively young. Nevertheless, it's easier to discuss their feelings as they get older. So, now is the perfect time to get into that habit. Ask your child how they feel. Most importantly, ask your child's opinion all the time.

Now, here's a secret: empower your child to decide as much as possible. Giving your child a chance to make decisions builds confidence. It also shows them you trust their judgment. Age-appropriate choices, such as what clothes to wear or what they'd like for dinner, can go a long way toward building confidence in your child within the safe and controlled environment you have provided for them.

In the next chapter, we'll dive deeply into connecting with your child at a deeper level. So, don't go anywhere because there's lots more heading your way.

[xxxiv] Maslow, A. H., Stephens, D. C., & Heil, G. (1998). *Maslow on management*. New York: John Wiley.

[xxxv] Ventegodt, S., Merrick, J., & Andersen, N. J. (2003). Quality of life theory III. Maslow revisited. *TheScientificWorldJOURNAL, 3*, 1050-1057.

[xxxvi] Sowislo, J. F., & Orth, U. (2013). Does low self-esteem predict depression and anxiety? A meta-analysis of longitudinal studies. *Psychological Bulletin, 139*(1), 213.

[xxxvii] Adler, R. F., & Benbunan-Fich, R. (2012). Juggling on a high wire: Multitasking effects on performance. *International Journal of Human-Computer Studies, 70*(2), 156-168.

[xxxviii] Killgore, W. D. (2010). Effects of sleep deprivation on cognition. *Progress in brain research, 185*, 105-129.

[xxxix] Vitale, K. C., Owens, R., Hopkins, S. R., & Malhotra, A. (2019). Sleep hygiene for optimizing recovery in athletes: review and recommendations. *International journal of sports medicine, 40*(08), 535-543.

CHAPTER 6

Finding that Deeper Connection

There is no such thing as a perfect parent. So, just be a real one.

- SUE ATKINS

We all try our hardest to be the perfect parent. We read books, listen to advice, or take classes. However, there is no such thing as being a "perfect" parent. Most importantly, your kids don't expect you to be perfect. They expect you to be there for them whenever they need you.

Throughout this book, we have focused on how to pull the reins on anger. We've learned how we can keep our emotions in check. Now, the time has come to focus on how we can connect with our children at a deeper level. That deeper connection involves being there for our children, no matter what.

Being there for our children involves providing them with the love, support, and protection they need to thrive in today's world. Above all, we seek to create a deeper connection with our children. This connection helps us recognize our children's needs instinctively.

Your instincts are what make you the perfect parent for your child. Unfortunately, the day-to-day grind might mess with our innate compass. So, we must strive to connect with our children beyond our usual routines.

This chapter unfolds how we can find that more profound connection with our children. We'll explore meaningful activities you can do to hit that next level with your children. Please remember that we don't have to be "perfect" parents. You must strive to be present parents—the kind of parents your kids need you to be.

Don't touch that dial! There's lots more heading your way.

Time to Ditch the Screen

Modern technology is nothing short of miraculous. The things we can do with a click or a swipe are unbelievable. Can you think back to when we didn't have these fantastic time-saving gadgets? I know. It's hard to think back to before smartphones, computers, or voice-activated devices made our lives so easy.

But there is a dark side to technology. The dark side is too much screen time.

According to a 2018 National Institutes of Health (NIH) study, children who spend more than two hours a day engaging in on-screen activities generally score lower on language and thinking tests.[xl]

Yikes!

According to Common Sense Media, this figure seems startling when we consider that most kids spend 2.25 hours of screen time per day.[xli]

Double yikes!

Dr. Jennifer Cross, pediatrician and developmental expert at the New York-Presbyterian Komansky Hospital, had this to say about children and too much screen time:

> *If your children spend most of their time engaging with an iPad, smartphone, or the television, all of which are highly entertaining, it can be hard to get them engaged in non-electronic activities, such as playing with toys to foster imagination and creativity, exploring outdoors, and playing with other children to develop appropriate social skills. Interaction almost exclusively with a screen would be like working out only your arm muscles and nothing else. You would have really strong arm muscles but at the expense of overall fitness.[xlii]*

I don't know about you, but that information blew my mind. You see, we don't believe that tablets and TV are harmful. If we monitor what our kids watch and do, we feel safe. However, too much screen time's effects go beyond unsafe content.

Becoming overly reliant on electronic devices stunts children's overall development. In that regard, we cannot afford to let our kids' growth become lopsided.

There's something else we need to consider here: the psychological impact that excessive screen time has on our kids. A fascinating 2018 study examined the association between screen time and psychological well-being.

Do you know what the study found?

> "Moderate use of screens (4 hours a day) was also associated with lower psychological well-being. Associations between screen time and lower psychological well-being were larger among adolescents than younger children." [xliii]

All right, so things are getting serious. What do the researchers mean by "lower psychological well-being?" Here's what they found: [xliv]

- Less curiosity
- Lower self-control
- More distractibility
- More difficulty making friends
- Less emotional stability
- Being more difficult to care for
- Inability to finish tasks

That's quite a handful! It's incredible how much damage a seemingly innocent device can cause to our children's psyche.

Furthermore, excessive screen time can lead to negative consequences such as impulsive, compulsive, unregulated, or addictive behaviors. [xlv]

Oh, yea... how many tantrums have we encountered every time we ask kids to turn off their devices... In fact, it's common to see kids hooked on their devices at the dinner table.

But it doesn't have to be that way.

So, here's my pitch to you: if you're serious about connecting with your children at a deeper, emotional level, it's time to ditch the screen.

Now, hear me out. I don't mean locking up your kids' phones and tablets. I suggest finding suitable alternatives to help keep your children away from screens. I understand that things haven't been easy over the last two or three years. After all, being at home most of the time enhanced our dependence on digital devices.

But now is the time to ditch the screens.

Don't get me wrong, mindful and regulated use of digital devices is linked with well-being.[xlvi] Using screen time positively can yield highly positive effects. But there is a fine line between healthy screen time and its unhealthy counterpart.

Is Too Much Screen Time Negative for Adults?

Indeed, too much screen time can have equally harmful effects on adults.

Think about it.

Don't we all spend just a little too much time on our phones and devices? I know you use your phone and computer for work and grown-up stuff. I get it. But then again, we might spend just a little too long on social media, streaming videos, or perhaps playing a fun game.

I mean, there's nothing wrong with healthy habits.

But when we spend a little too much time, we open the door to negative consequences. Here is some food for thought:

- Too much screen time can lead to obesity due to a lack of physical activity. Obesity is a precursor to diabetes, high blood pressure, and cholesterol issues.
- Sleeping issues are common effects of too much screen time. Blue light emitted from devices can cause disruptions in your brain's natural sleep cycles.
- Chronic pain in the back and neck can result from poor posture exhibited while on mobile devices and computers. Also, chronic pain stems from sitting too long and not getting enough physical activity.
- Depression and anxiety may settle in due to excessive screen time's adverse effects on people's emotional and psychological well-being..[xlvii]

That list above is quite a mouthful. I'm sure you can relate to some or perhaps all of these situations. So now imagine your children getting too much screen time. You get too much screen time. Your partner may also get too much screen time.

When do you get enough time for yourselves?

That's the challenge here. The challenge is to ditch the screen across the board. The aim is to get you and your kids to look away from the screen and focus on one another. When you focus your time and attention on the family, you can begin to relate at a much deeper level.

Plus, I have some news for you. In the next section, we'll look at how you drastically improve your relationship with your family with a few simple tweaks.

The Power of One-on-One Time

American actor and author Dave Willis once said, *"Time is the currency of relationships. If you want to invest in your relationships, start by investing your time."*

Wow, there's a lot to unpack there.

First of all, we must consider if our relationships are worth investing in. We must decide if it's worthwhile allocating resources to our relationships. If so, we must determine which relationships are worth our resources.

Time is the most valuable resource we possess. We cannot buy time. There is no way we can get more time. Once time has passed, we cannot get it back. This reason underscores why devoting time to our relationships is so meaningful.

Secondly, we know that investing in relationships with our kids is a top priority. We know that dedicating time to them is a no-brainer.

But here's something I'd like you to consider: dedicating time to your family doesn't mean sitting in the living room while everyone's on their phones. True interaction with your family is about spending quality time together.

If you really want to spend quality time, ditching the screen is a great place to start.

Thirdly, we must look at investing time to yield a future benefit. By definition, investing is about taking resources today and employing them wisely to obtain a benefit at some point in the future.

Do you see where I am going with this point?

If we invest time in our children, we can expect positive outcomes down the road. These outcomes can come in any number of ways. For instance, your bond will become much closer. You can expect more confident, self-sufficient kids. You will eventually see a decrease in the number of encounters as your communication becomes much more effective.

What's the secret to bolstering your relationships with your children?

Spending one-on-one time.

So, let's look at one-on-one time and its immense value.

The Value of One-on-One Time

In short, one-on-one time means giving your **undivided attention** to your child. This point means no distractions. No phones. No emails. No work. Just your child and you. That's it.

Sure, I get it. It's not easy to find the opportunity to dedicate one-on-one time to your kid. It becomes even harder when you have two, three, four, or more kids.

But trust me, it's so worth it.

Please remember that it's not about finding the time. **It's about making time.** You can use the time management techniques we discussed earlier to clear up spots in your schedule. Use these spots to spend quality, one-on-one time.

What can you do during one-on-one time?

Well, anything goes!

In particular, I would advise you to spend time doing activities your child loves. Speak their love language. It could be as simple as cuddling and talking and as fancy as a movie night. It ultimately doesn't matter what you do. The point is that you spend time together.

I read this quote that perfectly sums up the value of spending time with your kids, *"Spending time alone with them helps you get to really know your child. This approach makes them feel more understood. It also helps you look for common interests and ways to help motivate them on anything from homework to household chores."*[xlviii]

That's what I'm talking about!

Spending quality alone time with your children allows you to see who they truly are. You get a sense of where they're coming from. You can't have that understanding unless you invest in your relationship.

What outcomes can we expect as we invest time in our relationships?

Here they are:

- Stronger bond between parent and child.
- The child feels valued and appreciated.
- Reduces attention-grabbing behavior.
- Children see there are no favorites.
- Builds self-esteem and self-worth.
- Provides a model for good behavior.

There's one point I'd like to discuss further. Spending one-on-one time reduces attention-grabbing behavior. In other words, your child doesn't feel the need to act out to get your attention. They already have it. So, why misbehave if there's no benefit to it?

Can you see where I am going with this argument?

So, I encourage you to make time for your child starting today! Your investment in time today will pay off by reducing stressful encounters down the road. Think about it this way: it's like taking medication that will prevent you from getting sick in the future. Is that something you would do? Of course! It's something we'd all do.

The Benefits of One-on-One Time with Children

Let's take a look at the benefits you can expect when spending quality time with your children:

First of all, one-on-one time reduces behavioral issues. Yes, there is a reduction in attention-grabbing behavior. However, you can expect to see overall behavioral problems decline. You can expect to see improved behavior at home and school. Plus, you can expect them to feel less inclined to engage in risky behavior.

Improved mental and emotional health is a direct result of one-on-one time. When your child feels loved and appreciated, their mental and emotional health shoot through the roof. In turn, this results in improved self-confidence, academic performance, and physical development.

Spending quality time with your child improves overall physical health. Speaking of physical development, children in a stable emotional state are much healthier. A study found that children with unhealthy emotional states are 2.45 times likelier to become obese than their emotionally healthy peers.[xlix]

Above all, spending quality time communicates to your child that you genuinely care about them. While work and day-to-day situations may take up a significant chunk of your time and attention, spending quality time signals that your children are also a priority.

At the end of the day, it's much better to be proactive. Devote your time and attention to your child today. You'll reap the benefits soon enough. Plus, your child will get the head start they need to become independent, self-confident individuals.

Tips on How You Can Spend One-on-One Time with Your Children

So, the big question remains, how can you make time for one-on-one interaction? I'd like to share these pro tips with you so you can make room for one-on-one time.

To begin with, include kids in day-to-day tasks. We're not talking about chores necessarily. Daily tasks can be just about anything you do every day. Personally, involving my kids in my daily tasks allows me to teach them about the real world. Something as mundane as going to the bank can become a valuable life lesson while you spend alone time with your child.

Also, don't overlook the value of doing homework together. Homework can be a major pain point for kids and parents. So, why not make it a unique one-on-one activity? This activity is especially effective if your child struggles with a subject or assignment. By devoting your undivided attention to their needs, your child will see that you take their needs seriously.

You can boost your alone time by setting up a regular "date." By "date," I mean scheduling a regular occasion where you and your child spend time alone, no questions asked. For example, you can start small traditions such as going for a walk once a week or eating a special treat. Something as simple as going out for ice cream can have a massive impact on your child's psychological and emotional well-being.

Now, here's something interesting: surprise your kids! Yes, kids love surprises. Surprises don't necessarily mean gifts. You can surprise your kids with their favorite meal. Often, small surprises go a very long way.

Personally, I've found setting up a bedtime routine helpful. Children love routines. It makes them feel safe. I love the bedtime routine I have with my kids. It allows me to tell my kids how much I love them and what they mean to me. If your children have trouble falling asleep, why not use your bedtime routine to visualize their dreams? You can play soft music and guide their imagination to far-off fantasy land. This technique helps kids relax, focus, and eventually drift off into dreamland.

Additionally, please ensure to be disciplined with time. If you're in a time crunch, let your kids know you have a specific amount of time for an activity. For instance, you plan to play bingo for one hour. During this hour, nothing can interrupt you. In doing so, your time learns the value of following a schedule while allowing you to devote your undivided attention. Please remember that even 10 minutes of undivided attention is much better than hours of mindless interaction.

Now, not everything needs to be black and white. Bend the rules if you have to. Don't be afraid to bend the rule if the occasion warrants it. For instance, you may allow your kids to stay up a little bit past their bedtime if it means spending more time with your reading a book, talking about themselves, or completing a fun activity such as a puzzle or coloring book.

Lastly, ditch the screen! Get rid of your phone, tablet, or computer. You want to devote your undivided attention. So, "undivided" means no distractions. Your kids want to feel that you're really there.

At first, making time for your kids may not be easy. But I assure you that it will become much easier once you get the hang of it. So, please don't give up. The payoff will be so worth it down the road.

It's All About Positive Parenting

Families are dynamic, living entities with many moving parts. As a result, families change all the time. Therefore, we need to understand that as our families change, so as our parenting methods.

Where am I going with this?

We should shift our parenting approach as our kids grow up. We can't expect to treat our teens the same way as when they were toddlers. We have to get with the program as our kids mature and develop.

Think about it.

How has your parenting style evolved over time?

It makes sense to make adjustments as your children grow up. For instance, you cannot treat a teenager the same way you would treat a toddler. I know that may seem silly, but it illustrates how we must change with the times.

There are several factors involved in our family dynamics. There are social, environmental, biological, and behavioral issues that influence our family dynamics.[1] Thus, we must take the time to examine the patterns and dynamics in our home life. Putting our families "under the microscope" can help us uncover areas for improvement.

Consider this situation:

A mom I once spoke to discovered that her son's overly enthusiastic behavior (to put it nicely) was due to excess sugar consumption. Once she cut back on her child's sugar intake, his behavior improved significantly.

This example highlights positive parenting. This mom got to the root of the matter instead of "disciplining" her child. She discovered that sugar was the real culprit, not her son. In reality, no amount of punishment would have improved her son's behavior unless he stopped consuming too much sugar.

The core of positive parenting lies in connecting with your child. When you connect with your child, there's no need to punish your children. Instead, your children feel they can open up to you about whatever is on their minds. When you open your heart, your kids don't need to compensate for their negative emotions with unruly behavior. They can just open up to you.

So, why is positive parenting a great parenting approach?

Here is a snapshot of what positive parenting looks like:

First, positive parenting focuses on spending plenty of one-on-one time building a meaningful connection between parent and child.

Also, positive parenting uses the power of incentives and rewards instead of bribes. Positive parenting praises and rewards specific actions to acknowledge a child's appropriate behavior.[li]

Positive parenting addresses what parents can control. This approach helps reduce stress by narrowing parents' scope of action into areas that they can fully control. For instance, parents take proactive steps to help their children spot danger rather than worry about the risks out there in the world.

Parents with a positive mindset provide consistent and age-appropriate guidelines and consequences for the children's behavior. They don't talk down to their kids. They don't threaten. Positive parents understandably explain things.

A positive parent strives to use positive interactions to address inappropriate behavior. This approach steers away from yelling and accusing.

Lastly, a positive parent creates a positive environment where they can address their children's needs. This attitude helps maintain an appropriate balance throughout their kids' day-to-day interactions.

Personally, my philosophy has focused on maintaining a consistent, balanced approach. In other words, I say what I mean, and I mean what I say. I want my children to know that I am true to my word, whether offering a reward for a well-done job or punishment for inappropriate behavior.

Above all, I have worked my tail off to spend as much time as possible with my child. So, I'd like to share five crucial habits that have helped me foster relationships with my kids:

Let's begin by focusing on lots of physical contact. By "physical contact," I mean lots of hugs. We often overlook the importance of physical contact. We don't hug enough. Plus, activities such as snuggling at bedtime or first thing in the morning can go a long way toward helping your children feel loved and appreciated. So, here's a challenge for you: aim for 12 hugs a day. There doesn't need to be any particular reason. Just hug away!

Finding that Deeper Connection

The second habit I'd like to propose is: have fun! It's one thing to say, "it's bath time," and it's an entirely different thing to say, "it's time to go sailing to the depths of the ocean." Making routine tasks fun and creative can make a significant difference. So, try to incorporate as much fun and imagination as you can. Trust me, allowing your child to use their imagination at all times will help you better engage with them.

A generally delicate aspect of balance is transitioning from one activity to the next. It is crucial to connect before transitioning. Generally speaking, kids have trouble transitioning from one activity to the next. This skill is something we learn as we grow up. So, why not make it easier for your kids? Make transitions fun and easy. For example, hug your child if you're transitioning from playtime to dinner time. Tickle them as you lead them to the dinner table. Make a game out of washing your hands. It's the little things that make such a huge impact.

Also, don't underestimate the power of emotions. Personally, encouraging emotions is at the forefront of my parenting strategy. I know that emotional outbursts can be pretty complicated to handle. But that doesn't mean that you should encourage your child to repress their emotions. It's much better to acknowledge emotions by identifying them. If your child is angry, encourage them to say they are mad. If possible, help them explain why they are angry. Allowing feelings to the surface helps kids manage them. Lastly, helping children cope with their feelings using strategies such as breathing techniques significantly improves overall emotional management. Please don't forget to listen. Resist the urge to scold or lecture. Listening with empathy wins every time.

Now, here's the piece de resistance: savor the moment. Amid the hustle and bustle of today's world, it's easy to miss the beauty of life. So, savor the moment. Admire the sights. Stop and smell the roses. Enjoy delicious flavors. This philosophy helps calm things down so that you can all focus on what truly matters: enjoying the precious time you spend together.

The most important thing I'd like to stress here is being there for your kids. Even when you're not physically present, technology allows us to be there via video calls and FaceTime. When you are physically there, be there. Try your absolute hardest to let go of distractions. Getting rid of distractions means ditching your phone. You'll be so glad you did.

There's something else I'd like to share with you. Over the years, I've relied on three key positive parenting techniques. I'd like to share them with you now. These techniques will help you focus your efforts so you can get the desired outcomes.

Here they are:

1. Set limits on behavior by communicating to your child what is unacceptable. When your child crosses the line, don't immediately punish them. Instead, let your child know they crossed the line. Explain to them why their behavior is unacceptable. Then, outline what you expect them to do next time.

2. Give clear instructions when explaining your expectations. This approach is especially important with younger children. Younger kids have trouble making assumptions or inferences. So, be as clear as you can. For instance, "You know better than that" is too

vague. Instead, "It's not right to hurt your little sister" clearly communicates what you expect from your child.

3. Keep realistic expectations about your children's behavior. Kids will never get it right the first time. So, you must be patient with them. Allow them time to grow and make mistakes. They'll get it right eventually.

4. Most importantly, don't get angry. I know it can be frustrating to have to repeat yourself. But trust me. Take it slowly. Remember, this is an investment. Investments don't pay off overnight. When they do, they can pay off handsomely.

As you can see, positive parenting is a highly effective strategy. But there's one other compelling strategy I'd like to share with you: the power of decluttering. Yes, that's right! Let's look at how decluttering can shift your mindset from stress and chaos to calmness and connection.

The Power of Decluttering

Chaotic environments are never good for kids.
Think about it.

Toys everywhere. Noisy and disruptive surroundings. That's enough to drive anyone crazy. It also creates needless stress for kids. In particular, chaotic homes directly correlate with children's behavioral issues. A 2012 study concluded that household chaos contributed to children's disruptive behavior.[lii] It makes sense, doesn't it? But do we pay attention to it?

On the whole, chaotic environments begin with clutter. Messy and unorganized surroundings contribute to children feeling overwhelmed. As a result, decluttering is essential to creating a healthy environment for your child.

Messy and chaotic environments have effects on children that go beyond disruptive behavior. Children that grow up in cluttered homes struggle with language, have a harder time managing their emotions, and lag in their cognitive development.[liii]

What can we do about it?

The answer is to declutter. Decluttering your environment begins with a couple of simple tweaks. For instance, finding a place for everything is a great start. You can invest in bins, cubes, and racks to keep toys off the floor.

Please don't neglect the power of decluttering. After all, in the previous chapter, we saw how order could help you free up valuable time. The power of decluttering holds true across many areas. So now, let's take decluttering to the next level. We're going from a time-saving activity to bonding and connecting one.

Do you want to make the decluttering process a one-on-one time activity?

Pick up and organize toys as a fun activity. For instance, make it a contest. See how many toys you can pick up in one minute. Then, see if you can pick up more in the next minute, and so on. Transforming a routine task into a game is a great way to bond with your child while removing needless distractions from your environment.

I always say, "never underestimate the power of decluttering." Cleaning up and organizing can be the first step on your journey to building a healthier environment for your child and yourself.

One Last Thought

Now that we've explored positive parenting in depth, there's one more topic I'd like to discuss with you: how positive parenting can help you raise self-confident and independent children. Yes, that's right!

Positive parenting is the foundation upon which confident children become well-adjusted and successful adults. There is no magic formula to raising successful young adults. The "magic," if you will, lies in setting your children up for success. Laying that foundation begins with positive parenting.

In the next chapter, we'll explore how positive parenting is a precursor to raising independent children. As your kids develop their independence, their self-confidence shoots through the roof.

So, stay tuned because the next chapter is chock full of good stuff you don't want to miss!

[xl] New York Presbyterian (2022). What Does Too Much Screen Time Do to Children's Brains? Health Matters. Last Accessed: August, 2022. Available at: https://healthmatters.nyp.org/what-does-too-much-screen-time-do-to-childrens-brains/
[xli] *Ibid.*
[xlii] *Ibid.*

[xliii] Twenge, J. M., & Campbell, W. K. (2018). Associations between screen time and lower psychological well-being among children and adolescents: Evidence from a population-based study. *Preventive medicine reports, 12*, 271-283.

[xliv] *Ibid.*

[xlv] Kuss, D. J., and Lopez-Fernandez, O. (2016). Internet Addiction and Problematic Internet use: A Systematic Review of Clinical Research. *World J Psychiatry.* 6 (1), 143. doi:10.5498/wjp.v6.i1.143

[xlvi] Aziz Rahman, M., Hoque, N., Sheikh, M., Salehin, M., Beyene, G., Tadele, Z., et al. (2020). Factors Associated With Psychological Distress, Fear and Coping Strategies During the COVID-19 Pandemic in Australia. *Global. Health.* 16, 1–15. doi:10.1186/s12992-020-00624-w

[xlvii] Mosley, Aris (2020). The Negative Effects of Screen Time for Adults and Children. Last Modified: October 10, 2020. Available at: https://blog.valleywisehealth.org/negative-effect-of-screen-time-adults-children/

[xlviii] Pro Mom's Club. N.d. Last Accessed: August, 2020. Available at: https://promomsclub.com/the-value-of-spending-one-on-one-time-with-your-children-and-how-you-can-make-it-

[xlix] Anderson, S. E., & Keim, S. A. (2016). Parent–child interaction, self-regulation, and obesity prevention in early childhood. *Current obesity reports, 5*(2), 192-200.

[l] Repetti, R. L., Reynolds, B. M., & Sears, M. S. (2015). Families under the microscope: Repeated sampling of perceptions, experiences, biology, and behavior. *Journal of Marriage and Family, 77*(1), 126-146.

[li] Arzamarski, C. B. (2017). Catching kids being good: A practical guide to Positive Behavioral Interventions and Supports. *The Brown University Child and Adolescent Behavior Letter, 33*(11), 1-5.

[lii] Jaffee, S. R., Hanscombe, K. B., Haworth, C. M., Davis, O. S., & Plomin, R. (2012). Chaotic homes and children's disruptive behavior: A longitudinal cross-lagged twin study. *Psychological science, 23*(6), 643-650.

[liii] Hanscombe, K. B., Haworth, C. M., Davis, O. S., Jaffee, S. R., & Plomin, R. (2011). Chaotic homes and school achievement: a twin study. *Journal of Child Psychology and Psychiatry, 52*(11), 1212-1220.

CHAPTER 7
The Wings of Independence

The greatest gifts you can give your children are the roots of responsibility and the wings of independence.

- DENIS WAITLEY

Our entire discussion has led up to this point. Setting boundaries, establishing routines, managing anger and frustration, positive parenting, and one-on-one time all set the stage for raising independent children.

But what exactly do we mean by "independent" children?

Let's start by talking about what is not an independent child. Also known as a "contingent" child. They show the following traits:

- They depend on others' encouragement to carry out tasks.
- They rely on others for their happiness as they cannot take control of their emotions, actions, and thoughts.

- They depend on rewards and bribes, often attempting to discourage inappropriate behavior.
- They depend on others to make decisions for them as they lack the skills to make their own decisions, regardless of age..[liv]

Dependent children rely on others to manage every aspect of their lives. Fundamentally, contingent children cannot take ownership of their lives. They need someone (parents or grandparents) to manage their lives for them. In the worst of cases, dependent individuals require others to manage their lives down to small details.

In contrast, independent children show the opposite traits of contingent kids. Here is a look at how an independent child behaves:

- They show intrinsic motivation to carry out tasks and achieve their aims.
- They received guidance and support to explore activities of their choosing.
- They need very few rewards to carry out tasks and achieve their aims.
- They show good judgment since their parents gave them the opportunity to make their own choices even at a young age.[lv]

As you can see, independent children show good judgment in making their own choices. Independent kids can also do things without needing external motivation or rewards.

So, how can we foster independence in our children?

First of all, there is no magic formula. Fostering independence in our children boils down to providing them with an environment in which they can develop their personalities to the fullest extent. Let's take a closer look at what we can do to help build independence in our children.

The Importance of Play

Undoubtedly, play is a critical component in every child's development. Please bear in mind that "play" does not mean using digital devices for fun. Thus, we're not talking about playing with a phone, tablet, or computer.

We're talking about old-fashioned play using toys, games, objects, and above all, imagination. Imagination is a highly valuable component in a child's growth and development. Excessive screen time takes away from children's ability to use imagination to their fullest potential.

Specifically, playing alone allows children to explore their imaginations and personalities. It might seem counterintuitive, but solo playtime gives children room to grow and develop social interaction skills.

How so?

Playing along allows children to feel comfortable in their own skin. When alone, they don't have pressure to conform to peer pressure. For example, children can play with whatever they want. They don't have pressure from other kids to play a game they don't want.[lvi]

The benefits of solo play don't stop there. Here are eight key benefits derived from solo play:

- **Fosters self-entertainment**. Self-entertainment is a critical skill to develop. Kids who can entertain themselves don't need to rely on others to provide them with fun or enjoyment. As a result, self-entertainment helps build self-confident kids.
- **Bolsters imagination**. Solo play allows children to explore their imaginations freely. The lack of peer pressure gives children room to spread their imaginary wings in any direction they choose.
- **Builds social independence**. Playing alone removes group pressure. In particular, alone time eliminates the need to conform to group demands.
- **Develops calmness**. Playing in a group setting generates fun and excitement. While excitement and interaction are good, children also need downtime. Solo play allows children to develop calmness to offset extended periods of excitement and fun.
- **Fosters self-soothing**. Self-soothing gives children the chance to explore their emotions and solve problems themselves. In other words, solo play removes reliance on others to regulate mood and help deal with situations.
- **Gives space**. Parents can't be with their children 24/7, even if they want to. Solo play allows children to play on their own without feeling neglected. Independent kids look forward to both playing with parents and solo time.

- **Eases them into school.** Preschoolers almost exclusively interact with their parents. As a result, going to school may cause an abrupt shift in their social interaction. By allowing children to play alone, they realize that their parents won't be there with them 24/7. As a result, children can transition more easily into school and build relationships with others around them.
- **Gives parents space.** Spending significant chunks of time can be draining on parents. Now and then, parents need a break, too. Consequently, solo play affords parents some downtime. This downtime can then be used for any number of activities, including "me" time.

Indeed, solo playtime can give you a much-needed breather. Now, here's something to consider: please don't feel guilty about letting your kids play alone. I know that leaving your kids to play without you might seem neglectful. It would be if you ignored them. However, solo play time is not about ignoring your children. It's about giving them space. Solo play time, in turn, gives you some space. It allows you to get other stuff done so that you can spend even more time with them.

I know that might sound strange, but it's true. Imagine you get an extra half hour. What would you do with it? For instance, getting a head start on dinner can lead to an enjoyable meal with your kids. So, don't overlook the power of solo playtime.

Why Is Independent Play So Important?

OK, we've established that independent play is highly beneficial for kids. But why is independent play so important?

Here's the low down:

Independent play fosters self-reliance and self-regulation.

Think about that for a minute.

In the real world, we can't always rely on someone else to care for us. There comes the point where we need to deal with things ourselves. However, if we never learn how to do it, we can never become truly independent.

Do you see where I am going with this?

I'd like to share a quote from Cindy Bohrer, Director of Early Childhood at the Village School in Houston, Texas, "While quality interactions and playtime are essential for healthy relationships and development, children also benefit from opportunities to develop independence and self-regulation skills." [lvii].

This insight is quite fascinating!

First, independence is vital for building your child's overall personality. We've established how solo play scaffolds self-reliance.

Secondly, self-regulation, like self-soothing, is a cornerstone of independent adults. You see, successful adults don't need others telling them how to act or behave. They know what to do in most situations. That knowledge comes from having strong self-regulation skills.

Let that sink in for a minute.

Adults who don't learn self-regulation skills often have trouble grasping their actions and reactions. For example, those violent outbursts you see on videos result from people being unable to keep their emotions in check. Most of the time, these folks never had the chance to learn how to address their feelings properly.

Please remember that one of the most valuable things you can do for your children is to give them space. Under your watchful eye, allowing them to explore the world can do wonders for their overall development.

How to Encourage Independent Play Time in Children

So, the million-dollar question is, how can we encourage independent playtime?

The answer I propose to this question is a ten-step plan you can implement today!

You see, encouraging independent play time is a question of a mindset shift. There's no need to build a special playroom or purchase a bunch of expensive toys. All you need is to set the stage so your child can take full advantage of the situation.

If anything, I always tell folks to keep it simple. Setting up a simple play area is much better than an ornate one.

How so?

The more stuff around your child, the more they will become distracted. Keeping things simple allows your child to focus on the game at hand. Keeping things simple is the core of my ten-step plan.

So, Let's take a look.

To begin with, give children toys they can manipulate. Toys such as blocks, figures, cardboard boxes, modeling clay, balls, and stuffed toys, all of these so-called "simple" toys, give children an opportunity to interact with them. Highly sophisticated toys are cool and fun but don't allow children to manipulate them.

Also, please remember to choose age-appropriate toys. In other words, you want to ensure your kids play with toys that give them a challenge but don't require your intervention. As your children grow, you can purchase toys that provide them with increasing challenges.

Above all, a safe zone is critical for independent play. A secure area includes removing potential dangers such as covering electrical outlets or blocking off stairs. Some folks I've spoken to like to have cameras or baby monitors to keep tabs on their kids. A low-tech solution is to create a play area where you can keep a visual on your kids while you do other activities.

Please remember to ease into independent play. This is important, mainly if your child has never really played on their own before. You can start by spending 15 or 20 playing with your child and then get up to do something else. The first couple of times may be tough to get away. Your child may quickly notice your absence and call you back. The secret to this tactic is to allow your child to focus entirely. By allowing your children to immerse themselves in the game completely, you can gradually move away and let them play alone.

Managing your expectations is a critical point. You cannot expect your kids to play automatically on their own, especially if they've never done so. So, take it easy on them. Gradually work your way to total independent playtime. Your kids will eventually get there.

One strategy that's worked wonders for me is to lay things out for my kids. I tell them what we will do and how much time we will spend on it. For instance, I'd say, "Okay, you guys can play for the next 30 minutes while mommy takes care of something in the kitchen." Giving your kids parameters gives them the structure they need to know what will happen next.

To complement the previous step, it's helpful for you to stay close. This step is especially important when you have younger kids. Staying within eye and earshot allows you to step in if there's anything your kids need. I also find it helpful to pop in to check on them. Kids feel reassured and comforted when they see you, even if you don't do or say anything to them.

Here's a key consideration: when your children play alone, let them play alone. In other words, avoid interrupting them. Think about it... it's hard enough to get kids to focus. So, interrupting them may become quite counterproductive.

What do I mean by "interrupting" them?

Something as simple as commenting on their game can take a child's focus away from it. Getting your child to refocus on the game may then become quite tricky. Ultimately, it's best to leave your kids alone when they're alone.

Here's something else to consider: keep things fresh. Kids can get bored quickly when they play the same games or with the same toys. So, encourage your child to play with different kinds of toys. I like to build specific sets. Each set contains a group of toys that encourages my kids to try various activities. One set contains art supplies. Another set contains cars and trucks. Other collections include blocks, figures, furniture, you name it. The aim is to give your child the freedom to explore their possibilities.

Parents' common fear is what happens when kids get "bored." Now, I say "bored" because kids' imaginations meander in several unpredictable twists and turns. As such, predicting how long a child can spend playing a specific game is tough.

So, here's my advice: don't worry if your child appears to get bored. Allow them the freedom to play their own game. In doing so, you foster their independence. Some parents feel a need to step in as soon as their child gets bored. However, doing so actually restricts their freedom. Also, rushing in to address your child's boredom curtails their ability to self-regulate emotions. Let your kids explore their possibilities instead. Trust me. It might be a bit nerve-wracking at first. Ultimately, your children will become much more flexible to changing situations.

Lastly, make playtime a routine. You don't need to schedule it every day. But whenever you do, make sure it's on a regular schedule. If you can schedule 30 minutes, let those 30 minutes be actual independent playtime. If you can squeeze in some time every day, then so be it. Kids love routines. So, try your best to make independent play time part of a routine whenever possible.

Play Time Ideas

Now, I know what you're thinking: sure, playtime sounds fun, but what if I don't know where to begin?

Ah, I've got you covered!

Here is a list of the best ideas I've encountered throughout my experience as a mother and educator.

- Let's start with structured play. Structured play consists in playing a game following a specific set of instructions. For instance, the child puts together a model kit. Using structured play can be a great way to help your child reach a specific outcome. Please remember to give your child age-appropriate games and tasks.
- The flip side of structured play is unstructured or self-directed play. In this scheme, children are free to do whatever their imagination dictates. You can offer as much or as little guidance as you want. For instance, you can set a stage for your children to act out a puppet show. Also, you can give your kids the leeway to come up with their own ideas.
- Outdoor games are a great way to engage in structured and unstructured play. You can allow your children to run freely depending on the weather, space, and toys, among other factors. Otherwise, combining structured

activities such as arts and crafts in the backyard can give your kids the best of both worlds.

- Dress-up games are a fantastic way of giving your kid's imaginations freedom to roam. Kids can dress up and pretend they're anything they want to be. This activity is a great way for kids to explore jobs, community roles, and daily activities. For instance, kids can dress up in different uniforms and pretend to do all kinds of jobs. After, they can tell you what jobs seem most appealing to them.

- Music and dancing games are great for active kids. Do you remember musical chairs? Games like that allow children to explore sound, music, rhythm, and physical activity. Your kids can play with musical instruments and let their imaginations fly.

- Sports are an excellent way to engage in structured play. At first, you need to ensure they understand the game's rules. Once they've grasped the rules, you can let them play freely.

- Puzzles, memory, board games, and cards are all great examples of structured play. Board games help unleash imagination while stimulating a host of cognitive skills. I highly recommend board games. Although, you may need to try a few until you find the ones your kids truly enjoy.

- Hobby and craft kits are great, especially for older kids. For instance, painting cars and dolls give kids maximum freedom to explore their imaginations.

Remember, please avoid screen time as much as possible. We've discussed how much we need to divert kids' attention away from screen time. While I'm not saying you should strive for zero screen time, minimizing screen time is always a great rule of thumb. Use solo playtime for physical and mental exercise. Your kids will be much better off in the long run.

Positive Parenting and Independent Children

It seems like we've been building up to this moment, right?

Yes, that's right. Positive parenting has a direct influence on raising independent children.[lviii]. In essence, positive parenting focuses on empowering kids. So, what could be better for independent kids than positive parenting?

While the relation between positive parenting and independent kids is clear, there are five key strategies I'd like to share with you:

First of all, don't do everything for your kids. In short, don't do anything for your kids if they can do it themselves. Of course, many activities require training and practice. But once kids can do an activity independently, let them do it. They will feel empowered and in control of their environment. For instance, give kids space to do homework on their own. You may need to help them first. But as they gain confidence, you can back off gradually.

Also, allow your kids to contribute. Everyone plays a key role. So, let your kids contribute in any way they can. Something as simple as picking up toys can become a valuable contribution. The most important thing is to acknowledge their actions.

Positive words can go a long way toward boosting your kids' self-confidence.

Please don't forget to allow room for decision-making. You'd be surprised to find out how many parents don't give their children enough room for decision-making. Allowing kids to make age-appropriate decisions is critical to boosting their self-confidence and independence. Think about it. Making decisions is a crucial trait of independent people. So, why not foster decision-making skills in your children?

It's essential to encourage effort and hard work. Encouraging your children to work hard for their goals is one of the most valuable lessons you can instill in them. However, please ensure not to punish failure. Often failure is part of the learning process. So, it's always a good idea to turn failure into a learning experience.

Above all, don't shy away from encouraging problem-solving. Our first instinct as parents is to facilitate things for our kids. But there are times when we need to let them figure things out for themselves. One of the best things you can do is guide your kids with problem-solving skills and strategies. Other times, you need to let them try and try until they figure things out. Try your best to encourage your kids to think in terms of possibilities. In other words, encourage them to figure out how to solve the problems they encounter during play and in their lives.

Please remember that you're a valuable guide. Your role is to give your kids the tools they need to solve the challenges they face.

Give your kids every chance to feel empowered. They'll be much better off for it.

Final Thoughts

Raising independent and well-adjusted adults is our main focus. Indeed, raising self-confident kids is not easy. But now, more than ever, we have the luxury of knowledge and experience on our side. So, I would encourage you to take this discussion and internalize it. I know that we've covered quite a bit of information. That's why I would like you to take the time to reflect on the wait we've talked about.

Ultimately, I am confident your heart is in the right place. As parents, we want nothing but the best for our kids. But there's one last thing I'd like you to remember: please ditch the guilt. You're doing your absolute best to create a peaceful and loving environment for your kids.

Your kids cannot ask for more.

Your best effort is what your kids need and deserve. So, don't feel guilty if things aren't perfect. Nothing is.

I want to thank you for the hard work you do. I know you feel like there's more you could do. But you know what, every day is a new opportunity to grow. Growing little by little, day by day, will lead you to the best place you could have ever imagined.

[liv] Taylor, Jim (2010). Parenting: Raise Independent Children. Psychology Today. Last Modified: November 17, 2010. Available at: https://www.psychologytoday.com/us/blog/the-power-prime/201011/parenting-raise-independent-children

[lv] *Ibid.*

[lvi] Duncan, Apryl (2021)- Why Playing Alone Is Important for Children. Last modified: February 24th, 2021. Available at: https://www.verywellfamily.com/why-playing-alone-is-important-3129415

[lvii] Patel, Ojus (2019). Stop the Mom Guilt. It's OKAY for Your Child to Play Alone. Last Modified: Octobrer 3rd, 2019. Available at: https://theeverymom.com/experts-agree-independent-play-creates-successful-adults/

[lviii] Haine, R. A., Wolchik, S. A., Sandler, I. N., Millsap, R. E., & Ayers, T. S. (2006). Positive parenting as a protective resource for parentally bereaved children. *Death studies, 30*(1), 1-28.

CONCLUSION

Wow! Doesn't it seem like we just got started?

We have been through a fantastic journey of self-discovery and personal fulfillment. I know that it's not easy to tackle some of these issues. After all, it's never simple to talk about the things that affect you so much.

I also know that anger, frustration, and even disappointment are emotions we need to deal with constantly. It's never easy, but we can make things less taxing on ourselves.

We have discussed various ways to deal with life's stressors. Most importantly, we've discovered what causes our reactions. These discoveries have paved the way for a new sense and direction in our lives.

The most significant achievement in this book has been uncovering how we can handle relationships with our kids. Nothing is more valuable than our kids' lives and futures.

So, what's next?

Now that we've presented all these tools and insights, it's time to get to work. It's time to roll up our sleeves and make the most of everything we have learned here. I would greatly encourage you to go back to any section you feel you need to further your understanding, reflection, and analysis.

I would also like to encourage you to listen from the heart. I know you do, but please listen to your heart, especially during those tough times when nothing seems to go right. Those are the most difficult times to find focus and settle on life's most precious things.

Trust me. It's not simple, but if I can do it, you can. Please take the time to observe your feelings and reactions. Concentrate your efforts on taking a proactive approach. Nipping issues in the bud will make tackling your everyday life easier without feeling overwhelmed.

Lastly, I'd like to leave you with a small reflection.

In my experience, I've learned that guilt doesn't lead anywhere. Guilt only fuels our negative emotions. Nevertheless, we feel guilty about the things we wish we could do.

But let me tell you that we're not perfect!

There's only so much that we can humanly do. We have limitations. Time and energy can only go so far. Please ditch the guilt. Instead, focus on the things you do right. Think about how much you do for your family and the things you get right every day.

What about the things we don't get right?

No worries!

We can always work hard on improving those aspects.

Never forget that you got this. You can do anything you set your mind to.

Conclusion

Thank you once again for taking the time to read this book. If you've found it helpful and informative, please tell your friends, family, colleagues, and neighbors about it. I'm sure someone else out there will find it useful, too.

Made in the USA
Columbia, SC
02 April 2025

56034324R00089